Bernie Whitebear

Bernie Whitebear

An Urban Indian's Quest for Justice

LAWNEY L. REYES

The University of Arizona Press » Tucson

The University of Arizona Press
© 2006 Lawney L. Reyes

⊗ This book is printed on acid-free, archival-quality paper.
Manufactured in the United States of America
11 10 09 08 07 06   6 5 4 3 2 1

Library of Congress Cataloging-in-Publication Data
Reyes, Lawney L.
Bernie Whitebear : an urban Indian's quest for justice /
Lawney L. Reyes.
p. cm.
Includes bibliographical references and index.
ISBN-13: 978-0-8165-2520-1 (hardcover : alk. paper)
ISBN-10: 0-8165-2520-X (hardcover : alk. paper)
ISBN-13: 978-0-8165-2521-8 (pbk. : alk. paper)
ISBN-10: 0-8165-2521-8 (pbk. : alk. paper)
1. Whitebear, Bernie. 2. Senijextee Indians—Biography.
3. Indians of North America—Washington (State)—Social
conditions. 4. Indians of North America—Services for—
Washington (State) 5. Indians of North America—Washington
(State)—Politics and government. 6. United Indians of All Tribes
Foundation (U.S.)—History. I. Title.
E99.S546.W497 2006
979.7004'9794—dc22
                                        2005028812

Dedicated to

Mom and Dad

Family and Friends

Contents

Foreword

I have seen many American Indian leaders of note in my now lengthening lifetime, but none like Bernie Whitebear. I first met Bernie when I was an impressionable young Indian attorney fresh from law school in the early 1970s. Much later, in the 1990s I had the opportunity to work with him more closely as the Director of the Smithsonian's National Museum of the American Indian, where Bernie served ably and faithfully as an early Trustee of the then-nascent institution.

In both cases Bernie had long been a legend, but in each instance he evidenced fundamental characteristics of personality and spirit that endeared him to me for a lifetime—and that, in my own humble way, I try always to emulate. Bernie was a person of high intelligence who thought quickly and well in all circumstances and in the face of often challenging situations. His intelligence was cool rather than heated in nature, which gave him uncommon control in the most trying of times.

But a cool intelligence should never be confused, in Bernie's case, with any lack of passion for his work and commitment, and this characteristic, indeed, defined him for me. It was this very combination of an intelligence of the mind driven by the passion in his heart that set Bernie apart from other distinguished luminaries in the contemporary Native community.

A second aspect of spirit and personality, however, combined with Bernie's passion and intelligence, and it was the reason that even those who differed with him strongly still always loved and respected him. Bernie had an unfailing sense of personal grace, compassion, and understanding in all situations, including those very adverse in nature. To me this countenance emanated from his very nature and reflected a gentle soul much at ease with itself.

With the passage of time and the evolution of my own path through life and profession, I take note of those Native leaders, like Bernie, who marked and even defined important moments in the histories of the first people of the Americas, and who worked tirelessly and self-lessly, with strong hearts and gentle spirits, on behalf of their community. I am honored to have walked, while I could, beside this man, Bernie Whitebear, because I loved and admired him—and always will—for who he was and what he did for us.

W. RICHARD WEST
Director
National Museum of the American Indian

Preface

What is it that compels a person to do unique things in life? Why would one fervently devote a life to changing something that is so firmly entrenched? What gives a person the determination, the power, and the ability to do this? These questions are sometimes asked of people who do remarkable and measurable deeds. There have been many theories but no firm answers to explain this. Each case seems to be different.

Perhaps early conditioning is the answer. Maybe the individual involved had inherited the right genes from ancestors that gave the ability to observe needs and achieve things differently. Maybe he or she was blessed by some power with the ability to right things that are wrong. Then again, perhaps that person had no choice but to try to change conditions that were unbearable. Perhaps it is necessary to suffer then survive difficult times, inflicted by others, to understand injustices and know what has to be done to right them.

Whatever the answer, Bernie Whitebear accomplished deeds and won victories for his people that no other Indian accomplished. He crossed into political territory normally off limits to his people. Bernie gained access to foreign areas that no other Indian leader entered. He did this continually for forty years. During his time he gained the respect of many from different walks of life and varied ethnic and social backgrounds. Bernie amassed thousands of friends and supporters in the Northwest and throughout the nation. He became one of the most popular and well-loved leaders in Seattle. He was given dozens of awards, and many tributes were held in his honor. The press loved him, and wrote dozens of articles about him. Along the way, there were those who differed with him on points of view, but no one held this against him. There was always an aura of respect surrounding Bernie. Eventually, everyone he met became an admirer or friend. He was always recognized as a person who strived to improve the quality of life for those less fortunate than himself.

For these reasons, I decided to write the life story of my little brother.

"I believe this little one is destined to do
good things. One day he will go to help The People."

—Cashmere St. Paul, Sin-Aikst elder

One for All

The Depression was in its eighth year, and people throughout the country were experiencing hard times. Everyone searched desperately for ways to survive. Jobs were hard to find, and people could only measure existence from day to day. Families were hungry and left their homes traveling to other states in the hope of finding new lives. Some, who could not restore good times, ended their struggles by ending their lives. Many who were once well off became dirt poor. The effects of deprivation showed in the eyes and faces of almost everyone. Thin frames, almost skeletal, replaced the once robust and healthy bodies of many. It was now a life of futility and a way that projected little hope for the future. The hopelessness was evident as each tried merely to survive the day, hoping that other days would be better.

For centuries the Sin-Aikst People had lived along the Columbia River near the Canadian border and north into British Columbia. They lived on a vast and beautiful land base heavily forested with many lakes and streams. Wildlife, fish, and especially salmon were abundant, and the best roots, berries, nuts, and herbs grew from the land. The People were blessed to live in an environment that allowed freedom; they enjoyed life and moved about unhindered.

When the white men came, life began to change. The People were soon corralled onto smaller parcels of land. They were forced by the U.S. government to share land with eleven other tribes. They faced even harder times when the whites came in to claim their land as settlers. The People had been subjected to a controlled and impoverished

I

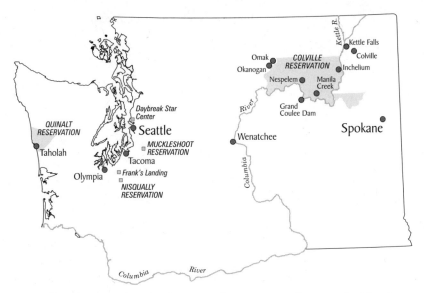

Map of Washington showing locations that were significant in the life of Bernie Whitebear.

lifestyle for over a half-century before the Depression hit the rest of the nation. Those hard years of deprivation and struggle had hurt them, but it also toughened those who were able to survive.

Hard times for the Sin-Aikst first came early in the 1800s with contact of the white man's disease smallpox. Within months this disease reduced the number of the people in the tribe from two thousand to fewer than four hundred. With the loss of warriors and tribal leaders, The People lost their strength and could not resist the forces of white settlers who came to take their land. This was followed by the establishment of the U.S. Army at Fort Colville near the Columbia River to protect the interests of the whites, who were settling the area at an alarming rate.

The Sin-Aikst lost large tracts of land over a short period of time. Soon miners came, with the blessing of the U.S. government, to exercise their options to this reduced land base. The miners were given the authority to move The People about in the areas where they lived. This allowed them to search unimpeded for gold and other minerals of worth. The disemboweling of hillsides and mountains left eyesores everywhere The People now lived.

A short time later the Columbia River was being poisoned with zinc, arsenic, lead, mercury, and other hazardous materials from a smelter in Trail, British Columbia, just north of the Canadian border. The People were unaware of this, and years would pass before anyone learned of the dangers.

In 1935 a foundation of steel and concrete was placed to hold and anchor the Grand Coulee Dam. This structure blocked the traditional migration of salmon in the Columbia River and prevented forever all salmon from going upriver to spawn. The dam destroyed the major food source for the Sin-Aikst and other tribes that had fished for salmon at Kettle Falls for centuries. Salmon fishing had become a part of their lifestyle. As time went on, it became the central part of their culture and influenced their beliefs in the spiritual powers. Kettle Falls and the salmon that leaped the falls to go upriver to spawn directed the pattern of life for the Sin-Aikst. The life of the tribe revolved around the great Chinook when they appeared in June every year.

The Sin-Aikst and the Swhy Ayl Puh (the Colvilles), their close friends and neighbors, had traditionally been the caretakers of Kettle Falls and supervised the sharing of salmon with the various tribes that came every summer. Before the taking of any salmon, the Salmon Chiefs of both tribes stood in the shallow parts of the river below the falls and gave thanks to the salmon as they swam up to leap the falls to go upriver.

After the tribes lost Kettle Falls, they barely managed to survive. Hunger and poverty became commonplace. The tribes affected were forced to change their traditional ways that they had enjoyed for centuries. When the Columbia River rose to cover Kettle Falls, it also covered land that contained the best roots, berries, nuts, and plants that The People had used for medicine and a variety of other needs. The Sin-Aikst, like other tribes throughout the United States, were reduced to mere images of who they once were.

It was into this world that my little brother, Bernard Reyes, was born on September 27, 1937, at the Colville Indian Agency Hospital in

Nespelem, Washington. Bernard was the third child born to my mother, Mary. She had named the baby after her beloved uncle, Chief James Bernard, of the Lakes Indians in the Kettle Falls area. Chief Bernard had died of a heart attack in 1935, before Bernard was born. James Bernard had led his people well for nearly thirty years. He had traveled to Washington, D.C., three times to negotiate a reservation land base and fight for the rights of his people. He was loved and respected by everyone in the tribe. Mom's uncle had descended from his uncle, Chief Kin-Ka-Nawha, who descended from his uncle, Chief See-Whel-Ken, who was chief of the Sin-Aikst from the early 1800s to 1860.

My dad, Julian, stood and looked into the eyes of his newborn son. "Look at the little one, Mary. He resembles a baby eagle. His hair is unruly as if he had just hatched from an egg. His nose is hooked and his eyes look fierce, just like an eagle who is hungry and searching for prey." Mom smiled as she studied Bernard and nodded her head in agreement. She had always maintained a love of wildlife, and especially eagles, whom the Sin-Aikst believed had special powers.

Before Mom left her room in the hospital, she wrapped Bernard carefully in a blanket, allowing a portion of it to expose his face. She looked at my sister, Luana, and me and asked, "What do you two think of your new little brother? Isn't he a fine looking baby?"

I remember the excitement my sister and I felt when we first saw Bernard. He seemed so tiny to us. Neither of us had ever seen a newborn, and he captivated us. Luana and I assembled Mom's belongings into a paper sack and handed it to Dad. We followed him outside. It was a clear sunny day, and the air was brisk as we walked to the parking lot where the Model T waited. Luana and I climbed into the back to sit with Pickles, our small, black-and-white, shorthaired Boston terrier.

Pickles wagged his tail, curious of the newborn addition to the family. Mom sat in the front seat holding Bernard. Luana was very excited about having a baby brother. She sat close behind Mom watching Bernard's every move. Luana had never had a doll. Her baby brother would become her doll, to play with, care for, and love. Luana became protective of Bernard at the early age of four. Now, at six, I would have to be protective of two people, my sister and now my little brother.

Dad opened the driver's door and adjusted the gas and spark levers behind the steering wheel. He walked to the front of the Model T and grasped the handle of the crank and yanked it upward. The motor gasped and then took hold. The family traveled the gravel-surfaced road, stirring a trail of dust as we headed to the small town of Nespelem, a few miles north.

He took the Cashe Creek Road east to reach the San Poil River Valley. This was beautiful country, with the river flowing through a heavily forested area of fir, tamarack, and ponderosa pine. One could smell the fragrant evergreens and undergrowth that lined the river. Near the top of the mountains that bordered the valley to the east, heavy boulders formed ponderous cliffs. Here and there they were spotted with fir and pine. The Model T traveled north for a few miles, then turned east and crossed the river at Bridge Creek. It labored up the tree-covered mountain range to reach camp, twenty miles away, near the Gold Mountain summit.

The elevation was nearly forty-five hundred feet, and the air was thin and brisk. The camp was located at the junction where the Gold Mountain Lookout Road joined the main road leading to Inchelium. Bernard's first home was made of sheets of canvas, sewn together by our dad.

The Colville Tribe had hired Mom and Dad as fireguards that summer. Their job was to stop visitors and advise them where to camp. During the summer many white people came to the Colville Reservation to fish and vacation at Twin Lakes, about seven miles below and east of the summit. They gave advice to visitors on how to care for campfires to prevent the accidental outbreak of forest fires. When the weather was hot and there was little rainfall, forest fires could be set easily, endangering the millions of acres of forests on and about the reservation.

Bernard received constant attention at the Gold Mountain camp from each member of the family. When he was not nursing, Luana played with him. Because there were no toys, she found things left by nature like pine cones, pine needles, rocks, or pieces of wood and bark that had an unusual design to them. Luana presented these for Bernard to look at. Pickles would come up and check on Bernard while Mom held him. After inspecting him, Pickles would lie down next to Mom. He seemed to understand that he now had to protect Bernard as well.

At bath time the baby was placed in a large metal pan in the open air. Bernard enjoyed baths and the attention he received. After his bath Mom wrapped Bernard tightly in his blanket and gently massaged his nose. Then she pinched his nose firmly at the bridge to shape it. The Sin-Aikst Indians had always done this to give their children an aquiline shaped nose. Mom told us that Bernard, as young as he was, resembled her father, White Grizzly Bear (Pic Ah Kelowna).

Within a few weeks the weather had cooled noticeably and the air during the morning hours carried the chill of fall. In the morning we could feel the brittle cold when cookware was handled to prepare breakfast. Because of the change in weather, my parents' work as fireguards had ended. It was time to move on.

The canvas shelter was taken down and folded. Dad placed it on top of the cab of the Model T and secured it with rope. Our food, bedding, lanterns, and cooking utensils were loaded into the back of the car. The camp area was checked for any debris left on the ground. Pickles inspected the campsite for one last time then ran to the Model T and jumped in through the front door for the trip to Omak. The family was hopeful we would find work picking apples in the orchards.

Dad drove down from the Gold Mountain summit on the winding gravel road. Along the way deer appeared several times. Some stood and watched with long, alert ears while others loped gracefully out of harm's way. Grouse flew quickly to trees a safe distance away. Rabbits sat ever watchful alongside the road. They darted to safety in the bushes that lined the road as the car approached. Our family had traveled this road many times, and the Model T sensed its way down from the summit.

"We'll take the Cashe Creek Road to Nespelem and head for Omak over the Desautel Pass," Dad told everyone. "It will take maybe five hours to make the trip." We children remembered the way because we had made the trip before, in 1935 and 1936.

It was midafternoon when we reached Omak. Once the Model T had crossed the masonry bridge that stretched over the Okanogan River, the Colville Indian Reservation was left behind. We were now in "white man's country." This was where the apple orchards were, and this was where our family would go in search of work. After crossing the bridge, Dad took a right turn onto Main Street. White people were everywhere, and no Indians could be seen. We were not welcome on this side of the river.

As we drove through the middle of town, the whites stopped what they were doing and looked upon us as intruders. At the end of town Dad turned left and the Model T climbed to the upper benches above Omak, where hundreds of acres of apple orchards sprawled to the adjoining hills. Dad drove the Model T a few miles further and turned into a dirt road that led to a large house. There were several cabins and sheds surrounded by acres of apple orchards. A tall white man in overalls came from the house and talked with Dad. He pointed to a small road that led into the orchard.

"We have a job," Dad said enthusiastically. "We'll set up camp down the road in the orchard, close to where we'll work." He drove to the edge of the orchard that followed a barbed wire fence, close to where we would pitch our canvas shelter.

Mom and Dad spent the following days picking apples, and Luana and I were given the responsibility to care for Bernard. Mom periodically came to nurse Bernard and check on us. Pickles assumed his duty as watchdog and caretaker.

One day, as Mom and Dad worked close by, a pickup truck drove by. Three young men were seated in the cab and four were standing on the bed enclosed by wood rails. When they saw our parents on their ladders they started shouting obscenities. One of them yelled, "What are you redskins doing on white people's land?" Another shouted, "You Siwash are so stupid you can't tell a tent from a tepee. By the looks of that rag shelter you live in you must not know what a real tent looks like." As they drove past another shouted, "Go back to your reservation, no dirty Injuns allowed on white people's property." They drove away laughing.

Mom and Dad were angered by the treatment, but they ignored the insults and continued to work. They were concerned about the safety of us children. At night Dad placed a 32.40 Winchester close to where he slept, within easy reach. We children were puzzled by the treatment from the white men. Our family had not experienced this type of behavior before. We were apprehensive and determined to keep a close eye on Bernard. We did not want him to be harmed. Pickles seemed wary as he stood watch at the entrance of the tent.

"Mom, what does 'Siwash' mean?" Luana asked, with hurt and concern showing in her eyes.

"It's a bad word used by white people who do not like Indians," Mom answered.

Dad became angry every time he heard that word. He had come from the Philippines in 1912, when he was only seventeen years old. Dad could not speak English then, but he was fluent in his own language, Tagalog, and in Spanish. He had experienced prejudice when he first arrived in Seattle. Dad learned to tolerate the attitudes and behavior of white people directed against him and others who were not white. He wondered why white people had felt it necessary to invent hurtful words to describe those who were nonwhite.

After marrying Mom, Dad made many friends while living on the Colville Indian Reservation. Everyone accepted him as one of the tribe. Mom was only seventeen when I, their first child, was born. Dad was thirty-six. When the white men had called Mom a Siwash it angered my father. He wanted to fight back and defend his wife, but he was totally outnumbered. He reasoned that it was the best strategy to endure the humility to protect his family from any harm. Dad decided to keep quiet and accept the abuse.

During our stay at the orchard, the family experienced daily harassment from the white men as they drove by the camp area. Sometimes, other young whites joined to add more insults. At times profanity was used to make things worse. Mom was further demeaned when one called her a "stupid squaw." Although there was no physical harm used against our family, we all sensed the hatred of the white men. Our family was apprehensive and could not enjoy the time spent at the orchard. Luana and I kept close to the shelter with Bernard. Pickles was always nearby, ready to defend, if necessary.

The apple harvest finally ended. The three weeks spent at the orchard had seemed endless. Dad took down the shelter and folded it carefully as he had done so many times before. All our food and possessions

Julian and Lawney
Reyes, Portland,
Oregon, 1931.

were packed into cardboard boxes and placed in the back of the car. The
owner of the orchard paid Dad in cash for the boxes of apples that had
been picked. We were all relieved we were going home to Inchelium to
be among friends and relatives again. Our family had tired of the abuse
by the white people. We were unaware that there was more abuse to
come.

Dad drove the Model T north alongside the Okanogan River toward
Tonasket, Washington. He wanted to take the highway to Republic,
then down the San Poil to Bridge Creek. We would take the road east
over Gold Mountain to finally reach Inchelium alongside the Columbia River.

Before our family reached Wauconda, we stopped for a rest alongside
the highway. Pickles jumped from the Model T. He was attracted to a
smell in the middle of the highway, and he went to investigate. A car

could be seen in the distance traveling very fast. I tried to call Pickles, but my friend did not hear me. Four white men riding in the car purposefully ran over him. We were in shock as the car sped on to Tonasket.

We dug a shallow grave and buried Pickles alongside the highway. I tied together a cross of two small sticks with twine and handed it to Luana. She pushed it gently into the soil of the little grave. Luana and I prayed quietly as tears streamed down our faces. Afterward our family climbed into the Model T, and we proceeded sadly on our journey home to Inchelium.

The little town of fewer than three hundred people lay along the west side of the Columbia River in the eastern part of the Colville Indian Reservation. As we came into town, several people walked about and rode horses. Horse-pulled wagons moved down the street, stirring small trails of dust. Other wagons, with tethered horses, were on both sides of the street. A few cars were parked here and there, but they were uncommon. Only a few people in town could afford one.

During the winter horse-drawn sleighs replaced the wagons. Only the jingle of small bells tied to the harnesses of the horses could be heard as they pulled the sleighs quietly through the snow. This complemented the quiet atmosphere of the little town of Inchelium.

The town water pump stood in the center of the Main Street. The pump was the sole source of drinking water for those who lived in town. All day long people could be seen cranking and filling a bucket to satisfy their needs. The pump also served as a meeting place for those who wanted to visit and exchange news. Sometimes, during the summer when the weather was hot, children took turns cranking the pump while others put their head under the spigot to get wet and cool off.

The name Inchelium came from the Swhy Ayl Puh language; it meant "where the small waters meet the big water." The town was located on the Columbia River where Hall Creek and Stranger Creek flowed into the river. The town was surrounded by a forest of pine, fir, and tamarack. It was usually a quiet setting except for the caws of crows and the chirping of blackbirds. During the day, meadowlarks sang clear melodic tunes. At night coyotes were heard in the distance. Sometimes, an owl hooted from trees nearby. But the only sound that was constant was that of the Columbia River as it flowed powerfully south.

There was a small ferry docked at the river that carried cars to the community of Gifford that was off the reservation. This allowed people to travel to Kettle Falls and north to the city of Colville on an asphalt highway.

In the fall of 1937 I entered my first year of school. While I was attending school Mom took Luana and Bernard for walks about town visiting relatives and friends during the day. Sometimes they went to the river and walked along the shoreline. Luana helped Mom push Bernard in a small buggy that had been borrowed from friends. On weekends I would join them.

"The salmon used to go up the river by the millions," Mom instructed us. "They were on their way to their spawning grounds above Kettle Falls. That's where The People would catch the salmon, dry them, and store them away."

Mom would stop and rest when we reached a large rock alongside the river. "Other tribes fished Kettle Falls also, the San Poil, Couer d'Alene, Okanogan, Spokanes, Nespelem, even tribes from the Plains," she continued. "Those Indians would bring dried buffalo meat and robes made of fur to trade for the salmon. The Sin-Aikst and the Swhy Ayl Puh would make sure every tribe received their fair share of the salmon. Food was plentiful in those days and everyone was happy."

At other times we went into the general store about a block away from our small wood-framed house. The store served as another social center in Inchelium. Sooner or later everyone in town or visitors from out of town would go to the general store to visit and exchange news. Mom usually sat by the pot-bellied stove, where she spent time visiting with friends. Old apple boxes and blocks of wood provided the seating. Bernard was content in his borrowed buggy, and Luana was always about the store looking at all the merchandise.

Old Cashmere St. Paul entered the general store one day. The weather was getting colder. I watched as he walked to the pot-bellied stove and held his hands out to receive warmth, then rubbed them together briskly. Cashmere usually sat outside the general store on Main Street watching everything that went on. Now that it was colder, he came into the store to thaw out.

Cashmere was a tall man and dressed in his usual attire. The high-domed brown reservation hat with its eagle feather sat prominently on his head. Long gray braids hung almost to his beltline. He wore a buckskin vest with fringes at the back, which covered a homemade cotton shirt that was always buttoned at the neck. Old worn denims with patches at the knees covered his slightly bowed legs, and buckskin moccasins encased his feet. Cashmere was in his eighties, and everyone in Inchelium recognized him as an important elder, one-time hunter, and would-be warrior. He always carried an old white cotton flour sack over his left shoulder that held a .45 Colt semi-automatic pistol.

Cashmere nodded to those seated at the stove. He nodded to Mom and stepped over to look at Bernard lying in the buggy. Cashmere acknowledged Bernard with friendly eyes. He never smiled, but his eyes lit up if he liked something or was in a good mood. He was especially pleased to meet the grandson of Pic Ah Kelowna. Cashmere and my grandfather had hunted and fished many times at Kettle Falls and above where the Kootenay River joined the Columbia.

Cashmere whispered, "This young one comes from good people. A long time ago there was Chief See-Whel-Ken, after that Chief Kin-Ka-Nawha, then Chief James Bernard. They were all good men. His grandfather was Pic Ah Kelowna. He was a great hunter." Cashmere drew closer to the baby. "The little one resembles him. See his eyes and nose. We were Sin-Aikst then. We were a strong people with much land and food. We believed in the Great Spirit and all the other spirits. I believe this little one is destined for something good. I believe that one day he will help The People."

I listened as he talked to Bernard. The old man fascinated me. He had a special look about him, the wrinkles on his face, how he walked, how he talked and carried himself. Cashmere knew forthcoming changes would not be good for The People. He had witnessed the smaller salmon runs at Kettle Falls. He knew that white fisheries at Astoria, Oregon, near the mouth of the Columbia River, were the cause. This made survival difficult, and there was never enough food. The traditional ways of gathering food were changed, and this upset the traditional patterns of the tribe.

The great homeland of the Sin-Aikst was lost. At one time it followed the Columbia River from Kettle Falls to about one hundred miles north of Revelstoke, British Columbia. White people had taken the land and passed laws protecting it for their own use—protecting the land from Indians, the rightful owners. Now the people were on the verge of losing their last common possession, Inchelium. It would soon be covered by water. The Columbia River would rise with the completion of the Grand Coulee Dam and cover everything, including the great Kettle Falls.

Shortly before Cashmere's birth, Chief See-Whel-Ken died. During his time as chief the Sin-Aikst were strong. There was plenty of food, and the tribe followed its traditional ways. See-Whel-Ken became chief in the early 1800s, and he lived a long life. Before his time, the Sin-Aikst were divided into two groups. The Upper Sin-Aikst lived to the north in what is now British Columbia. Their land base started where the town of Trail is and reached north through Castlegar and Nakusp to about the Revelstoke area and north, where the Columbia River bends south and flows to the lands where the river originates. The Lower Sin-Aikst lived in what is now Washington. Bands were in the area where Northport, Bossburg, Marcus, and Kettle Falls now stand. They also lived along the Kettle River where it joins the Columbia River and up where the small towns of Boyds, Barstow, and Orient now stand.

When the Lower Sin-Aikst acquired the horse in the early 1800s, they became nomadic and were able to reach the plains to hunt buffalo, east of Missoula on the Great Plains. When the hunters got their buffalo, they cut the meat with the grain, placed it on racks, and dried the meat in the sun and wind. They also scraped the buffalo hides and rolled them so they could be tanned and smoked later by the women of their tribe. The tanned hides were used to cover their tepees or made into moccasins and shields to protect warriors. Sometimes the fur was left intact, and warm robes were made to cover people and bedding during the cold months of the year. The Sin-Aikst favored the buffalo hides because they were thicker and heavier than the deer hides they usually tanned and used. Their method of living changed as the tribe became nomadic. They no longer lived long in one place, and they adopted the tepee as their home.

The Upper Sin-Aikst lived for the most part as they always had. Because their land base was heavily forested and not suitable for horses, they relied on a special type of white-pine bark canoe for travel. The ends of the canoe sloped gently to the surface of the water to reduce wind resistance. It sat low in the water and was very stable.

Over the years the Upper and Lower Sin-Aikst kept in touch by visiting. One of the best times for gathering was in August during the huckleberry season. At these gatherings many bands from the Upper and Lower Sin-Aikst came. Many gathered at Red Mountain, near Rossland, British Columbia, where the best huckleberries were found. Old friends met and discussed the events of the days when they were apart. It was during this time when the young would get to know each other. Sometimes marriages would result, so that the ties between the Upper and Lower Sin-Aikst would remain strong.

Chief See-Whel-Ken died in 1860. He had led his people well for a long time. He was respected by his people and trusted and liked by the white people who lived in the Colville and Kettle Falls area. Life for the Sin-Aikst was still good, but changes appeared as more white people came to settle the land. Because of this, the Sin-Aikst were forced into smaller areas and the traditional hunting grounds could not be used. White settlers were beginning to fence off lands that they claimed with barbed wire. This practice prevented the Sin-Aikst from following age-old hunting trails traditionally used to find big game. Because See-Whel-Ken had no sons, Kin-Ka-Nawha, his nephew, became chief when he crossed over to the spirit world.

Cashmere recalled that during Kin-Ka-Nawha's time little of the original tribe existed. Smallpox, Christianity, white fisheries, legislation of the provincial government in British Columbia, settlers, and miners had all taken their toll on the Sin-Aikst. The traditional patterns of life eventually disappeared, and The People, now hurt, were open to accept a new spiritual direction. The messages of the Blackrobes were gradually being heard and accepted. Many in the tribe, broken and poverty stricken, knelt and accepted Christianity.

Cashmere studied Bernard. He viewed him as the future. He spoke softly, "I hope you grow strong and are smart enough to deal with the white man. Remember they are many and cannot be trusted. They are the ones who have wronged us. Don't forget they are the trespassers on our land. They do not own it." I listened as Cashmere spoke to Bernard.

The look on his face was very serious. "If you remember the words and wisdom of your ancestors, See-Whel-Ken and Chief Bernard, it will help you." We could see that these thoughts weighed heavily on Cashmere's mind as he spoke.

One weekend when I was with my family, I noticed Bernard's sharp, dark eyes as they intently studied Cashmere's face. A special relationship seemed to have formed between the two. Every time Mom brought Bernard into the general store, Cashmere came and spoke to him. Sometimes, he talked softly in Sin-Aikst. Bernard always smiled when he saw Cashmere. He liked the old man with the big hat who came to talk to him. I could tell that the wrinkles on his face were of interest to Bernard. The two seemed to communicate without talking.

As 1937 came to an end, almost all of the talk around the pot-bellied stove was about the Grand Coulee Dam. Everyone was having a hard time accepting that the town of Inchelium would soon be covered with water. We all would have to move to higher ground. Although the people knew of all the problems they would face when the river rose, there were no clear solutions about how everyone would survive.

The salmon were now gone because the concrete-and-steel base of the Coulee Dam had stopped their progress upriver. Salmon had always been a principal food for the tribes, but now hunting became a necessary way of life. Deer became the main food source for the Colville and Lakes Indians in Inchelium. Because there were few jobs and little income, hunters had to be frugal. It became too expensive to hunt with large-caliber rifles because the shells cost too much, so lower-caliber rifles were now used. It also became important that shells were not wasted: the deer must be hit with the first shot.

It took months for the Columbia River to completely cover the small town of Inchelium. During that time Dad worked with others to move the graves from the old cemetery to higher ground. It was a difficult time because the graves of loved-ones brought back memories of better days.

As the river rose, most of the people began putting the homes that could be moved on log skids. The houses were to be pulled by small Caterpillars to sites up in the hills. As houses were pulled away, the town of Inchelium began to take on a somber appearance. In places the water from the river began to replace land. Some of the older and more fragile of The People had homes that could not be moved. Those people remained where they were for as long as possible. The rising water had to be waded through to reach them. Friends and relatives continually walked what was left of the town site checking on the welfare of those who were still there. Eventually, the entire town was flooded and the remaining residents moved to the mountains to live in tents or tepees. Everyone had to ration what little food they had. Many became sick and had to depend on the traditional ways of curing. Those who could not remember the herbs and plants used for curing suffered the most. It was a struggle to survive.

All for One

In mid-February 1938 Mom and Dad's small house was raised, set on log skids, and moved to the hills to a place called Number 4. It would later become a part of New Inchelium. Dad had selected a site of one acre that bordered a small creek known as Cobbs Creek. When our family reached our property we explored the land. Luana and I were excited when we discovered mountain trout swimming in the creek. Mom carried Bernard down to the creek and he smiled and pointed at the trout as they swam up and down the creek in front of him. The acre had several trees, and our house was positioned in an open space between them. The land was covered with high wild grass. Although everyone missed Inchelium, our family was happy with the new location at Cobbs Creek.

Dad spent long hours working on the house. Repairs had to be made because parts of our home were damaged in the move. Later Dad built a small shed to hold tools, parts of the Model T, and glass jars used for canning fruits and vegetables. He dug a cellar beneath the shed that was reached by wooden steps. It was cool in the cellar, which was used to store potatoes and other vegetables to keep them from spoiling after they were harvested. During the hot months Luana and I spent time in the cellar to avoid playing in the sun. We carried Bernard down the steps and spread a blanket on the ground for him to lie on. The three of us spent hours in there playing and entertaining each other.

One day friends drove up and brought a small puppy into the yard. He was light brown and his fur was full and fuzzy. When Bernard saw it, his eyes lit up and he smiled. The three of us were delighted to have a new puppy to play with. He reminded Luana and me of Pickles. The little one ran up to Bernard as he sat on his blanket and licked his face. Bernard held the puppy close and laughed. Luana asked if they could keep it. Dad consented, and Mom named him Brownie.

Our family enjoyed our new home site, but we began to miss the feeling of community we once had in Inchelium. All of us missed the visits with Cashmere at the general store. We missed the salmon, our most important staple. Later the elders of our tribe would learn that the best fields for camas, bitterroot, chokecherries, and serviceberries were lost when the Columbia River rose and covered them. Food would be hard to come by now. In time the Sin-Aikst language and customs would gradually be set aside as the new community busied itself in trying to survive in a new way.

In the spring of 1939, for reasons unknown, Mom left home. Luana, Bernard, and I were caught off-guard and puzzled at the circumstances that faced our family, but Dad did not share information with us. He continued to work alone on different projects about the property. The three of us could tell that Dad wanted his privacy, that he did not want to talk about the problems between him and Mom. As a result, the three of us formed our own protective world and became very dependent on each other. It was like we built an invisible shield to protect us from any harm. The shield first covered us at the apple orchard in Omak when the white men harassed us. As we faced adversity in the future, this protective shield would grow stronger.

One day as we played with Brownie near the gate to the property, a car drove up and Mom got out. She had tears in her eyes, and she embraced the three of us. She held us close to her for a long time.

"I had to leave you because I felt it best to live by myself. I think it will be better for your dad, also. It's necessary to work someplace else to earn money. I will probably move to Nespelem or Grand Coulee Dam." Mom picked up Bernard and held him close. "I will try to get a job during the summer with Harry Owhi in Nespelem. He usually has a hamburger stand during the Fourth of July celebration days. After that I will probably go to Grand Coulee Dam and work at Harry Wong's Restaurant. I'm going to have a house built for all of us to live in after

I make some money. When it's built, I'll come for all of you. We'll live together and be happy. It will take time, and you'll have to be patient."

Mom told us to be brave and to take good care of each other. She told Luana, "You will have to be Bernard's mother until I can come for all of you." Luana promised she would take good care of her little brother. I told her not to worry. I would watch over the family and take care of Brownie and feed him every day. Mom got back into the car and waved at us. She was crying as the car went down the road.

That year Luana and I kept our promise to Mom. We watched over Bernard closely. He was able to walk and he followed us everywhere. At this time the bond between us grew ever stronger. We were inseparable. The private world we created for ourselves provided the security we needed to cope with each day. We tended to the household duties, entertained ourselves, and helped each other. Luana and I tried our best to answer questions and console Bernard when he needed it. We taught him new things and kept him busy with work and play. Luana and I knew that if we kept Bernard occupied, he would not dwell too much on thoughts of Mom.

Taking over Mom's duties of caring for Bernard was difficult for Luana. She was only six years old, but she was determined. Every morning she washed him, combed his hair, got his breakfast, and helped him brush his teeth. Once a week she bathed him in the laundry tub. I helped her fill and empty the tub after Bernard's bath. She helped Dad prepare meals and encouraged Bernard to eat vegetables and other important foods that helped keep him healthy. Bernard never argued with Luana and was eager to do what was right. When Luana read to him or gave him instructions, Bernard listened attentively. He was eager to learn and cooperate. Luana and Bernard became very close during that time. Dad did not interfere with us. He felt it best that we learn to care for ourselves by trial and error as he had when he was young.

Although Bernard appreciated Luana's attention and help, at times he missed Mom very much. He asked where she was or when she would return. I understood his feelings and spent more time with him. We went to the creek, and I showed him the trout and taught him what I knew about them. I described the markings and explained the difference between rainbow and mountain trout. I showed Bernard my hooks and spinners, my sinkers and bait, grasshoppers and angle-worms. Bernard always listened attentively as I shared my knowledge with him. After fishing in Hall Creek, I brought the fish home and showed him how to clean them. Bernard told me he would like to fish in Hall Creek one day when he got bigger. I promised to take him when that time came, when Bernard was older.

Later that summer, when I was eight years old, Dad bought an old single-shot .22 Stevens rifle. He gave it to me and taught me how to load and unload it and how to clean it. Dad impressed upon me that a rifle could be dangerous. He told me to never point the barrel at any-one. Dad bought a box of shells and set up tin-can targets on the hill-side across the creek. By the time I finished shooting all the shells in the box, I had become fairly accurate at shooting the rifle. Dad allowed me to take it in the Model T when we traveled about the reservation. When we came upon grouse or rabbits, he instructed me on how to shoot them. From that point on, we had meat to go with the rest of our food.

Mom spent much of her time away from Inchelium. She had to sup-port herself and raise money to pay for a lawyer to advise her during a trial that was scheduled for May 1940. Luana and I had no idea that there was an impending divorce. Mom had tried to plead her case with Judge William C. Brown in Okanogan but to no avail. The judge told her that rulings about the custody of the children would be decided at the trial to be held in Republic, Washington, the seat of Ferry County.

The day of the trial was clear and bright but one could feel the brittle cold in the wind that lingered during the change of seasons. Now Luana and I understood that the trial would decide our future. It was diffi-cult for us because we loved both parents. To choose between the two would be impossible. There were no clear answers to the problems that faced us. Bernard, at first, was unaware of the problems but he began to sense that things were not right. When he saw Mom he was over-joyed and he ran to her. He had not seen her for two months and he had missed her very much. Dad stood to one side as we ran to Mom and embraced her. We all cried tears of happiness.

The three of us played outside the courthouse during the trial. Both Mom and Dad had lawyers to represent their cases and witnesses to vouch for their ability to care for us. The afternoon seemed to never end, as Luana and I awaited the outcome of the trial. We learned that Judge Brown had ruled in favor of Dad. He would take custody of us for the summer. The judge knew that Dad could not afford to care for all three of us, so he ordered that Luana and I attend an off-reservation Indian boarding school in the fall. He reasoned that by sending us to a boarding school, it would help ease the burden of supporting us. We would not realize the impact of this decision until later.

Bernard would stay with Mom's foster parents, Charlie and Eliza Hall. Dad would have Bernard only during the weekends, when he was not working. Judge Brown ordered that Mom would have visitation rights whenever she could get off work. He felt sorry for Mom but he did not feel that she could properly care for us and work at the same time. Judge Brown knew she had no work experience except for picking apples and waiting tables in restaurants. He felt that his decision was in our best interest. The decree was devastating to Mom, but she did not have the money to carry the fight further.

After the trial Dad stood at a distance once again as we said good-bye to Mom. There were tears again but not of happiness. These were bitter tears of regret and sadness. Luana and I knew we would never share a home again with our mother. Bernard sensed that something bad had happened but he was not sure how bad and how long lasting it would be. He would learn in later years that the close precious world he was born into and had once known was ended.

Now that Dad's legal responsibility was to care for us, he devoted himself religiously to this task. He worked tirelessly at any job he could find. He went to work for the Works Progress Administration near Inchelium. There were about three hundred men working to cut the trees and clear the debris from the land that bordered the Columbia River. This had to be completed before the water rose. Almost all of the workers were white men.

The water would soon completely cover Inchelium and the land about it when the Grand Coulee Dam was finished. The four of us lived in a tent and followed the Works Progress Administration camp to the various work sites. We played with Brownie and entertained ourselves as Dad worked nearby.

One evening near the end of August 1940, Dad broke the news to us.

It was time for Luana and me to go away to attend another school. He said it was far away in another state. The school was called Chemawa. Judge Brown had ordered this at the trial, and Dad could do nothing about it. He told us we should pack what clothes we had in a sack and be prepared to leave in a few days.

We were grief stricken when we heard the news. The night before we left, we talked quietly with Bernard in the bedroom. We wanted to prepare him for what was to come. "You will have to take care of yourself from now on," I said. "We won't be here to help you. We'll have to go away and we don't know how long we'll be gone."

With tears in her eyes Luana added, "Remember to do all the things I taught you. Eat all the food you can get and drink a lot of canned milk with water, the way I taught you." Luana put her arm around his shoulder. "Make sure you always brush your teeth, after every meal. And make sure you feed and give water to Brownie."

I could not hide the pain I felt but managed to speak, "Brownie and you will have to take care of each other from now on. Remember to always take him with you when you go to the creek. Take him with you when you walk the trails we made. Those will be your trails now. Take good care of them until Luana and I return."

As we talked Bernard could not keep the tears from welling up into his eyes. It was difficult for him to talk. He could only nod his head to show us that he understood. Bernard was only two years old and he must have felt as if his world was ending. He had depended on us since Mom left. We had lived in our own precious little world, always working closely together. We did not sleep well that night. I remember praying that the night would never end.

The next day Jess Tresseder drove up to the gate in his pickup. He greeted Dad and asked if Luana and I were ready to go. Jess was white and a long-time friend of the family. He had been hired by the Colville Tribe to take Luana and me to Nespelem. From there a truck was scheduled to take us to Chemawa, near Salem, Oregon.

Bernard was hurting inside as he watched us prepare to leave. Tears welled up in his eyes once more. We hugged him one last time before we got into the pickup. It was the hardest thing Luana and I had ever done.

Bernard asked, "Can I go with them, Dad?" He added, "I could sit in the back of the pickup and I could hang on tight so I won't fall out."

Dad put his arm around Bernard, "You will have to stay home now and take care of Brownie because they are going on a long trip. They're going to have to go to school and they won't have time to play with you." He said quietly, "Pray that your brother and sister will travel safely and God will watch over them." Bernard stood helplessly with Brownie by his side as the pickup drove away.

After Luana and I arrived at our new school in Chemawa, we were still deeply concerned about Bernard. Not long afterward, I received a letter from Dad. He told us that Bernard was having a hard time accepting that Luana and I were gone. He wrote that the day after we left Bernard sat listlessly at the kitchen table. He could not eat his breakfast because of the hurt he felt inside. Dad later overheard a short conversation Bernard was having with Brownie on the small porch of our house, "You and I will have to take good care of each other, Brownie, now that Luana and Lawney are gone."

Coping

As the days wore on, we received weekly letters from Dad. He wrote that Bernard continued to miss Luana and me very much. Bernard had no toys to help him pass the time, so he walked with Brownie to the creek and watched the trout swimming. At other times, Bernard walked about the property following trails made by the three of us. Bernard would enter the house and sit, deep in thought. At other times he sat on the bed where Luana had slept. Bernard seemed to have thoughts only of Luana and me. Dad knew we were deeply concerned about Bernard's welfare, but he told us not to worry. He believed that eventually Brownie's friendship would help to get Bernard through each day.

Luana and I learned that while at the Halls' Bernard spent most of his time indoors. They felt he was too young to be outside by himself. Because they were elderly and not in the best of health, the Halls preferred to spend their time in the living room listening to the radio. There were no toys for Bernard to play with, and it was hard for him to occupy himself. No children lived nearby, Dad wrote, and Bernard had no one to play with. He did his best to entertain himself. Bernard sometimes play-acted as if two or more people were talking to each other. This helped him keep his mind off Luana and me and survive the loneliness he felt.

We learned from Dad's letters that he had brought my old wagon to the Halls' so that Bernard would have something to play with. He filled it with pinecones, rocks, and limbs of wood. Sometimes, he added empty bottles or tin cans. Bernard used his imagination and pretended that the things in the wagon were school kids. Bernard spent hours pulling the wagon about the yard.

When Dad came to pick up Bernard for the weekend he was told, "See the wagon. It's a school bus, Dad. It's taking everyone to school. Lawney and Luana are sitting in the back." As he pointed to two rocks, Bernard said, "This is my brother and this is my sister." When I read this part of Dad's letter it touched me very deeply.

During that time in New Inchelium, everyone was having difficulty. There was little money on the reservation. Many had nothing, but others shared what they had with those in need. Everyone lived from day to day hoping the next day would be better.

There were only a few jobs, and everyone had to depend on hunting. The Grand Coulee Dam was near completion, and the river would soon cover the old town of Inchelium completely. The salmon that used to come up the Columbia River by the millions were gone. Luana and I learned that Charlie and Eliza Hall had no one to hunt for them, and they had little food to share with Bernard. Occasionally, though, friends would kill a deer and share part of it with them.

Dad was not a good hunter and did not have a horse that could take him to the mountains where most of the deer were found. He took work where he could find it, but all of the jobs were temporary. His income barely made ends meet. He wanted to pay Charlie and Eliza for their care of Bernard, but sometimes he didn't have enough money, and the Halls told him not to worry about it. They told him he could pay when he could afford it. He told us in one letter that Bernard went without good meals most of the time. He never had fresh milk. When Dad could afford it Bernard was given canned milk mixed with water, otherwise he drank powdered milk with water. Fresh vegetables were available only in the summer, and there was no fresh fruit. If it were not for the commodities Dad got at the agency, they could not survive. Sometimes he had to barter his work for food. When Dad was totally broke, friends gave him staples like beans, cornmeal, and macaroni. Sometimes potatoes were given if there was enough to go around and they were still good. It was difficult for Dad to take food from someone and not be able to pay for it, but there was no other way.

At the end of May 1941, Dad had good news for Bernard. Luana and

I would be coming home for the summer. Bernard could not contain himself. He shared the news with Brownie. He walked down to the creek with his two companions and told the trout the good news his dad had shared with him. His brother and sister were coming home.

A few days later, Dad and Brownie drove to the Greyhound bus station in Colville to pick us up. As we got off the bus, Brownie barked his greetings and ran around us in circles. He finally came to me and stood on his hind legs as he planted his front paws on my chest. This had always been our way of embracing.

With Brownie riding on the right front fender, his chosen spot, the Model T followed the highway to Kettle Falls. We approached the Columbia River and were surprised to see a new bridge. As we crossed the bridge, Luana and I both looked upriver. We could not believe what we saw before us. Kettle Falls was gone. The beautiful river we once knew was gone. A large, motionless body of water now covered the falls. It saddened us to view what had happened to our river. We sensed something important was gone, never to return.

"What happened to Kettle Falls?" Luana asked, wide-eyed.

"While you were away the Grand Coulee Dam was completed," Dad answered. "It caused the river to rise. Kettle Falls and all the land around it is underwater now. Inchelium is gone. Things around here have changed. It will never be the same."

As Dad drove south along the river, Luana noticed that she could no longer smell the familiar fragrance of the Columbia. There seemed to be no smell at all. The beauty that once existed had disappeared. It was as if the Columbia River and everything about it had died.

When we arrived at Number 4, Dad steered the Model T past the house. "We have to go up to the Halls' to get Bernard."

Luana moved closer to the window. "I can't wait to see him. It's been such a long time. I wonder if he still looks the same. I wonder if he'll remember me."

As we pulled into the yard we could see Bernard standing by the front door waiting for us. We could tell by the broad smile on his face and the sparkle in his eyes that he was happy to see us.

We noticed that Bernard was very thin. He wore bib overalls and there were patches on both knees. Holes in his shirtsleeves exposed his bony elbows. The toes of both shoes were nearly worn through. We were saddened by what we saw. Luana and I had suspected when we left for our new school that there would be little food for Bernard and we could see the results of the last nine months.

I whispered to Luana, "I'll fish and hunt every day so that Bernard will have enough to eat during the summer." We would both do our best to bring Bernard's strength back while we were with him.

We embraced Bernard and held him firmly for a long time. There were tears in our eyes. It was hard to believe we were together again. Those nine months had been a long time.

Brownie barked and ran around the three of us with his tail wagging furiously. Charlie and Eliza came out to join them. "Welcome home. It's good to see you two again. It's good that Bernard will have company. Bernard will be happy to have someone to play with during the summer. He has really missed you."

After leaving the Halls', the Model T approached the gate of our property. Bernard pointed toward our new home. "There it is, our new house. Dad and Jerome Quill built it for us. Isn't it nice? It's bigger than our old house. See that little playhouse, Luana? Dad and Jerome built that for you. Isn't it nice?" Earlier in the year Dad got a loan from the tribe to build the small house. The old one had been in poor shape since it was moved to higher ground. The tribe agreed that it would be better to build another house rather than go through the expense and effort of repairing the old one.

Bernard could not wait to get out of the Model T. He wanted to show us everything. "It's closer to the creek, too," Bernard continued. "There's a ladder you can climb to go up to the attic. There are two windows up there. You can look out at everything."

Bernard looked as though his eyes were searching for something. "There he is! Look! Over there! See Goat over there. Dad bought Goat so I would have more company to play with me."

Bernard ran to the animal and put his arms around the goat's neck. "Goat follows Brownie and me when we walk on our trails. You have to watch out because he will butt you with his horns, mostly when you're not looking." We could tell Bernard was enjoying being the center of attention. "You know what?" he continued. "Goat likes to eat paper.

See that ladder leaning on Luana's playhouse? Well, Goat can climb that ladder and walk on top of Luana's playhouse. He can also get back on the ground when he wants to."

"What's the goat's name, Bernard?" Luana asked. "What do you call him?"

"Well, he doesn't have a real name. Dad and I just call him Goat. He seems to like that name, so we just call him Goat."

As we walked to the house, with Brownie running ahead, Bernard kept staring at us. "You guys look different. You are both a lot bigger than you used to be."

Bernard pushed the back door open and proceeded to show off our new home. He was happy and excited. He ran to the front door and flung it open. The creek flowed by only fifteen feet away. "I really like our new house." Bernard climbed the ladder a few steps. "I like climbing this ladder a lot. It goes up in the attic. I like to look out the windows. Brownie can climb ladders now, too. Sometimes he goes up with me." Bernard stopped halfway up the ladder and looked down at us below. "Do you guys like our house? Do you guys want to climb the ladder with me?" We assured him that we liked the house a lot and, yes, we would like to climb the ladder. Bernard beamed.

That summer Luana tended to Bernard. The two spent hours playing together in her playhouse. She took him for walks about the property. They walked the trails, tramping down the grass as they went. She was amused to see that Goat followed them everywhere. They walked down to the creek and watched the trout swimming. Luana noticed the fish had grown.

Luana found an old newspaper. "Would you like me to read to you, Bernard? Would you like that?"

Bernard smiled and nodded his head. They sat on the bed in their room and Luana read. Bernard sat quietly listening to every word. He enjoyed having his sister read to him. She also shared some of the experiences she had during the last nine months in Chemawa. Bernard was curious about the boarding school. He wanted to know what Luana and I did there.

Luana answered each of his questions, "It's a place where there are a lot of kids. It's a big school and they come from many tribes, from all over the country. Chemawa is a long way from here. It's near a big city called Salem, and it's in another state called Oregon. Maybe I'll be able to take you there when you grow up. I'll show you the big building where I lived. It's called McBride Hall. Lawney lived at Brewer Hall. We didn't get to see much of each other while we were there."

"I would really like to see it," Bernard assured Luana. He continued, "Luana, I would really like to ride in the bus you guys rode in. Dad said the bus is big and can carry a lot of people. I have never been in a bus. The only thing I ever rode in is the Model T."

Bernard yelled to me, "Let's catch some grasshoppers and feed the fish. Do you remember how to do that?" We spent the rest of the day catching grasshoppers and wading in the creek while Luana, Brownie, and Goat watched.

Summer was passing quickly, but the three of us made every day count. We spent the days visiting and exploring our property. Sometimes Dad drove us to the new little town of Inchelium, where he treated us to bottles of soda pop. At other times he drove us to Twin Lakes to watch fishermen as they caught the large rainbow trout in their small fishing boats or up into the hills to Upper Hall Creek, where the long creek began. Once we crossed on the Gifford ferry and drove to Colville on the other side of the Columbia River. The highway was topped with asphalt and it was very smooth in comparison to the gravel road on the reservation side of the river.

Time went quickly, and we taught Bernard many things to help him understand and care for himself. During that summer I fished nearly every day at Hall Creek. I wanted to make sure that Bernard had plenty to eat. Luana searched for things to read, and Bernard devoted his full attention to her words.

Near the end of August, Dad told us that it was time to go back to Chemawa. When Bernard heard this, his customary smile vanished. He remembered how much he missed Luana and me the first year, and he knew that it would be more of the same.

The last few days before we left, Bernard stayed close to us. He came with us wherever we went, with Brownie and Goat following. He asked many questions, knowing we would take the time to explain and help him learn. Bernard vowed to himself that he would not cry when we left. He would endure his feelings privately. But the day we left Bernard had difficulty holding back his tears. As we embraced he stated bravely, "Say good-bye to Lawney and Luana, Brownie. We won't see them for a long time. You say good-bye, too, Goat."

We learned later, from one of Dad's letters, that it took a few days for Bernard to adjust to being alone again. Brownie and Goat helped to give him the companionship he needed. The three of them walked the trails together. He imagined his brother and sister were with him, talking and walking along with him. At other times he led Brownie and Goat to the part of the creek where it was not swift. Bernard would look into the clear water and see his reflection. It was like looking into a mirror. Bernard remembered that Luana had taught him to do this. Dad said that Bernard asked Brownie and Goat, "Can you guys see yourselves? Do you see yourselves in the water?" As he played it brought back memories of the two of us. It made him sad.

In another letter Dad told us that Charlie Hall, realizing that Bernard was having a hard time, gave him more attention. He invited Bernard to walk with him down to the creek to get water. Charlie let Bernard play at the creek for a while before they returned home. Charlie sat on the porch to be near Bernard as he played in the yard with Brownie and the old wagon. When winter came, Charlie put on his heavy coat, donned his wool cap with the earflaps, and stood outside. He smoked his pipe while Bernard played in the snow. Bernard appreciated the company that Charlie gave him.

In December 1941, Dad wrote again. He told us that the Japanese had bombed Pearl Harbor and that America had declared war on Japan. Bernard was very interested when he heard that we might be going to war with Japan. Dad said that when neighbors came to visit and talk about the war, Bernard paid close attention to what was being discussed. Bernard wanted to know who the Japanese were and why they bombed the U.S. Naval ships at Pearl Harbor. Everyone who talked to Dad believed that many of the young men in Inchelium would surely join the army and help fight the war. He said at least they would get three square meals in the services, which is more than what they got at home in Inchelium.

Dad wrote that as friends came to visit and discuss the possibility of war, they wondered how it would affect the people in Inchelium. No one was sure at the time. Bernard sat nearby with Brownie curled up beside him. He tried to comprehend what everyone was talking about. He wondered what would happen when war came. Since he had no one his age to communicate with, he learned to listen to adults as they discussed matters of interest to them. As time went on, their interests became his interests.

After a heavy snowfall, Christmas came. Dad wrote that few in Inchelium celebrated because most had little money. He took Bernard to the old Catholic Church near the agency to attend Christmas Eve Mass. He said the manger scene showing Christ in his crib fascinated Bernard. After Mass he and Bernard went home and let Brownie inside. Goat had already made himself comfortable in the small shed that he had built. Stacks of hay were placed to protect the animal from the crosswinds. Dad told us that he had also cut and sewed a large burlap bag to fit on the top of the goat's back and sides. He fastened it to his back with twine to help keep him warm. There were no presents to share, so Bernard got ready for bed. As Bernard knelt to pray, he wondered what Luana and I were doing for Christmas. He wondered if the two of us had a manger to look at.

Dad added in his letter that he put more wood in the stove, then took a big drink from the whiskey bottle. Before going to sleep they listened to Christmas carols on the radio as he smoked his pipe. Bernard's words were slow but to the point as sleep approached. He said he hoped that "you and Luana would have a Merry Christmas. Bernard hoped God was watching over you and that you would come home safely someday soon." Dad wrote that Bernard was growing into a very thoughtful boy.

"He was interested in traveling to
different places and learning about new things.
Every day was an adventure."

—Julian Reyes, father

Exploring

On May 1, 1942, Dad wrote another letter. He had contacted George Whitelaw, who ran a logging outfit in Keller, Washington, asking for work. A week later George wrote to say he had a job for Dad as a brush piler, if he wanted it. The job did not pay much, but at least it was a job. Dad accepted. He wrote it was better than nothing.

After delivering Goat to the Halls for safe-keeping, Dad and Bernard traveled the Bridge Creek Road past Gold Mountain to the San Poil and finally to Keller. They stopped at the small town of one store and a gas station and asked for directions to Manila Creek. They came to three houses with some sheds and a barn. A pickup truck and two large logging trucks were parked in the yard, and a Caterpillar was parked in the large shed. Dad and Bernard drove up to the house as a heavy-set man with gray hair walked out. The man waved and called out that he was George Whitelaw. He asked if Dad was Julian from Inchelium. Dad answered yes and introduced Bernard and Brownie.

George asked how things were in Inchelium. Dad told him that everyone was barely making it from day to day, but, other than that, everything was as well as could be expected. Dad added that since the Columbia rose and covered Inchelium, everyone lived up in the hills and lower mountains now. He told George that no one saw much of each other anymore and that a lot of young men had left and joined the armed services.

When George Whitelaw learned that Dad and Bernard were to live in a tent, he gave them directions to a place to camp near a small creek that would provide good drinking water. That evening, after supper, Dad had some great news for Bernard—news that Bernard had been anticipating for months. Luana and I were returning home.

A few weeks later Dad and Bernard traveled to Wilbur, Washington, to pick us up. After they arrived at the train station, Dad told us, Bernard shielded his eyes with his hands and looked down the railroad tracks as far as he could. He did that until we heard the train whistle blow in the distance.

Luana and I could see Bernard as the train came to a stop. We could see that Bernard was very happy and excited. When Luana and I got off the train, Bernard ran to us and embraced us for a long time. The three of us were very happy as we stood there. Bernard stepped back to look at us.

He bent down to pick up a few rocks from the gravel on the tracks. "I can throw rocks a long way. Watch me." Luana and I watched Bernard throw about a dozen rocks down the tracks. "What is it like to ride in a train?" Bernard asked. "Sometime I would like to ride in a train. It looks like it would be a lot of fun. I bet it goes very fast."

Bernard had grown, but he was still very thin. He studied Luana and me closely. "You guys look different. You look bigger. Every time you guys leave and come back, you get bigger." Bernard looked at our clothing and shoes. "Your clothes look new and your shoes are very shiny. How did you get your shoes so shiny?"

"You have to use shoe polish," I answered. "We'll have to get some and I will show you how to polish your shoes." Bernard, still fascinated with the gleaming shoes, bent over and touched them gently.

As we traveled to Manila Creek, Bernard talked incessantly. He had much to share with Luana and me. "Brownie is tied up at camp. He's protecting it." Bernard warned, "You have to be careful at camp. There are a lot of rattlesnakes. They can bite you. If you're not lucky they can kill you." Bernard's face became serious. "If you see any rattlesnakes you should call Brownie. He knows how to handle them." He added, "Dad and I saw one by the creek the other day. It was very big and you could hear it rattling. When they use their rattles it sounds like something buzzing." Bernard looked out of the window and then continued his lecture. "I will show you where the rattlesnakes are. They are in the bushes along the creek. They like to stay in the shade. They do not like to be in the sun too long. Remember, if you leave them alone, they will leave you alone. When we get to our camp I will show you my rattlesnake pole. I use it to check for any rattlesnakes that might be hiding in the bushes. It comes in pretty handy sometimes."

Bernard's attention was distracted for a moment by a meadowlark sitting on a fence singing. "Meadowlarks sing pretty songs. I like to listen to them." He continued rambling, "Dad and I have lived at camp for two weeks. There are a lot of birds and animals at camp. At night you can hear crickets and frogs. You can hear coyotes singing. One time I heard an owl. Lawney, there are a lot of grouse you could hunt. We brought your .22. We will have a lot to eat now that you are home."

As the Model T descended to reach the ferry, Bernard pointed to the Columbia River far below. Luana and I were impressed with the view. From up high we could see the winding grade that finally reached the sparkling blue river. We always had a strong attachment to the Columbia River and always felt good when we were near it. As we descended, Bernard continued to instruct us of our new surroundings.

The large ferry carried us across the Columbia. It was larger than the ferry at Inchelium, and it traveled faster. Luana advised Bernard that this was the same river that flowed past Old Inchelium. He had not thought of this before. He remembered what Mom had told him about the salmon that went up the river before the Grand Coulee Dam was constructed. Now there were no salmon and much of the beautiful land, including Kettle Falls, was covered by water. Bernard remembered Mom saying that because of the Grand Coulee Dam the old ways of the Lakes Indians were destroyed. Bernard, at four years of age, could not comprehend the loss of the culture of the tribe, but he could understand the loss of salmon and wondered about that.

We drove up a narrow dirt road to find our campsite. Luana and I saw the canvas shelter in a small open area surrounded by trees. It was about forty feet away from a small creek.

Brownie became excited when he saw Luana and me. He started barking and trying to get loose from the rope that held him. I ran to him, and Brownie stood and planted his front paws on my chest. "Brownie is really happy to see you guys," Bernard said.

I untied Brownie before he ran to Luana. She picked up a stick and threw it, and Brownie ran to fetch it with his tail wagging excitedly. We had played this way many times in the past. Bernard watched happily. The broken bond of the past was mended as we played.

Bernard showed us around the campsite. He showed us the small creek and how water was taken and stored near the canvas shelter in two large glass bottles. "We put milk in jars with a lid on them. That keeps the flies and bugs out. There are really a lot of bugs around here. They get into everything." It was obvious Bernard was enjoying his role as instructor. "The jars are put in the creek to keep cold. We get the milk from a farmer who lives down the road. He's a nice man. His name is Mr. Campbell, and he has two kids, Irene and Gordon. They are very nice to me, and I think you would like them. He has horses and pigs. Mr. Campbell even has chickens, and we get eggs from him." Bernard was pleased to be able to hold the attention of Luana and me with the information he provided.

Bernard took us into the canvas shelter. "This is our bed. You have to check to make sure no rattlesnakes are under the blankets." Bernard raised the blankets carefully and peeked under them. "When it is hot they like to crawl under the blankets to keep cool."

As Luana listened to Bernard, I could tell by the look in her eyes that she was alarmed at what she was hearing. "If we found a snake, what could we do about it?" Luana asked, trying to maintain her composure.

"Get Brownie. He knows how to handle them," Bernard said, as he echoed our father's advice.

"Now, this is the stove Dad and I made." Bernard reached out his hand and touched the stove. "I helped him cut it in half. It was hard work but we did it. You can put wood in it to make a fire. You can cook food on it. Dad put a damper in the stovepipe. He says that makes it really hot. I was the one who put the stovepipe into the hole after Dad cut it out with a chisel. We found that stovepipe by the old house down the road. We tried it the other day, and it works pretty good."

Bernard said that he helped Dad set up the canvas shelter when they arrived from Inchelium. He helped move boxes of food, cooking utensils, and other necessities into the shelter. Bernard said that while they were doing that, Brownie inspected the area. When the shelter was up

Dad went up into the woods and chopped branches from the fir trees. He brought them to the canvas shelter and spread them on the ground inside. "We put burlap bags and then blankets over the branches. This is where we are all going to sleep when it gets dark. The upper bunk is for you, Lawney. The rest of us will sleep on the ground."

Dad gave Bernard a small bucket and asked him to go down to the creek to get some water. I went with him as Brownie ran ahead. Bernard saw movement in the grass and yelled that he thought he saw a rattlesnake crawling. He pointed to bushes along the creek and told me that it crawled into them. Dad found a long pole and poked into the bushes several times. We heard a buzzing noise. Dad told us that a rattlesnake was in there. He cautioned us to be careful.

Bernard was wide-eyed. Rattlesnakes fascinated him. Dad pulled the bushes apart so we could see the snake clearly. Bernard studied it for a long time as it remained coiled and continued to rattle.

Dad told us that rattlesnakes rattle to warn that they are there. Bernard ran to get his rattlesnake pole. He returned and poked it into the bushes. He wanted me to listen to the snake as it rattled. After studying the snake for a few minutes, we returned to the canvas shelter.

Supper that night was canned salmon and boiled rice with apples for dessert. Dad made coffee for himself, and he added a bit of whiskey to his cup. He stood drinking as he surveyed the campsite. He looked at the three of us, and I could tell he was very pleased. When it got darker, Dad lit the kerosene lantern and a soft glow covered the area.

That night we got ready to retire in the shelter. After I had climbed up to my bunk, Bernard came over and lifted a canvas flap. He told me that it could be raised if it got too hot in the shelter. He told me that it was like air conditioning. As I lay there I thought of Chemawa with indoor plumbing, electric lights, and warm comfortable bedding. The fir branches and burlap bags that served as our bedding were very uncomfortable. It was difficult for me to get to sleep. I looked down at Bernard. He was nearly asleep. The bedding did not seem to deter Bernard. He never complained. He had always had a positive attitude about everything. It was good to be home.

As we breathed the sweet fresh air, we listened to coyotes howling in the distance. Bernard told us earlier that Manila Creek had coyotes just like Inchelium. He said that he liked listening to them. It sounded like the coyotes were all singing. We heard crickets and frogs by the small creek. Bernard said a prayer for all of us before he fell asleep.

The next morning Dad went to work. He carried his axe, a file to sharpen it, and a water bag. The three of us followed him. Brownie ran ahead with his tail wagging. Bernard carried his rattlesnake pole, and we carried paper sacks with peanut butter and honey sandwiches and apples. A piece of salmon was wrapped in paper for Brownie's lunch. I thought to myself that we must have looked like a small army marching off to war.

It was a nice sunny day, and we were anxious to see where Dad worked. After walking a mile we came to an area where many trees had been cut. They were lying everywhere. Dad told us that he had to cut the branches off all the fallen trees. He instructed us to play with Brownie in the clear areas away from the bushes. He told us to keep an eye out for rattlesnakes and keep Brownie close by. Dad told me that I could help him pile the limbs of the trees after he had cut them. Bernard and Luana were to stay in the shade when it got hot, and everything would be fine. He told us that he should hang the water bag in a tree in the shade to keep it cool. Bernard and Luana were not to wander off.

When Bernard and Luana were not exploring the area, they watched chipmunks and squirrels running on logs or up in the trees. They chased red-winged grasshoppers and tried to catch them. They had watched me do this often. Bernard remembered it was my favorite bait for fishing. When the day got hot, Bernard and Luana drank from the water bag and sat in the shade with Brownie, watching Dad and me work. They watched as red-tailed hawks glided gracefully in the sky high above. Bernard wished he had wings and could fly as easily as them.

During their time together, Luana taught Bernard many things. She was pleased to see how bright he was. Bernard expressed a strong desire to learn, and she prepared him to read and understand numbers. As the two sat in the shade of the tall pine and fir trees, she shared information with Bernard as Mom had done before our parents' divorce. Luana and Bernard discovered later that the pinecones the squirrels carried were full of tasty nuts. They spent hours taking the nuts from the pinecones and putting them in a jar. The nuts became a favorite snack for us that summer.

Luana explained everything she knew about nature. Bernard always listened attentively and remembered everything she shared. She identified trees in the area and taught Bernard the name of each one. She did the same with insects and birds that inhabited Manila Creek. Luana's teaching would help Bernard when he entered school a year later in Inchelium. Her teaching would have a strong impact on Bernard when he grew older. Luana was only nine years old, but she was blessed with intelligence beyond her years.

In the fall of 1942, Luana and I went to school in Keller. There was a car that came to pick us up, along with three other children. I was now in the sixth grade and Luana was in the fourth. Dad had received permission from Judge Brown in Okanogan to do this. He had written that he could support us now that he had steady work and the school in Keller was a good one. The Summerlins, an elderly couple who lived about a quarter mile from our family's camp, cared for Bernard while Dad worked and Luana and I were in school.

Dad had visited the old small house where he had found the stove-pipe. The house looked as if it had been abandoned for years. It was in poor shape, but winter was coming and we knew we could not survive the cold living in the tent. We went in, cleaned it out, and made what repairs we could.

To bide his time while Luana and I were at school, Bernard played alongside Manila Creek with Brownie. Sometimes he tried to fish with my pole. He was now five years old, and he felt that he could do many of the things that I did. As the weather got cold, there were no rattlesnakes to worry about because they were now hibernating. When Luana and I returned home from school each day, Luana spent time reading some of her schoolbooks to Bernard. He looked forward to this time.

There was much snow that winter. It became very cold—so cold that Dad could not work for over two months. Bernard stayed at home with Dad during that time, and he enjoyed playing in the snow. He played outside rolling small snowballs into large ones, as Dad chopped piles of firewood during the daylight hours. Sometimes he walked out into the open field and made trails in the snow as Brownie followed close behind him. Bernard helped pack the firewood and stacked it near the front door of the house. When it began to get dark, he would come into the house, join Dad, and listen to the radio.

There seemed to be a lot of news coverage of the war. Bernard was curious about what was going on. He was beginning to form a connection with the bombing of ships by the Japanese the year before. One afternoon he told Dad, "It sounds like we are in a very big war. Where are they fighting now?" Dad did his best to describe the Pacific Ocean and the islands where the battles were taking place. Dad told Bernard that we were also fighting against the Germans in North Africa across the Atlantic Ocean. Sometimes he made rough drawings on paper hoping Bernard would understand.

Our food supply began to run low that winter, and we had to ration what was left. I fished in Manila Creek until it froze. Even then I fished in places where no ice covered the creek and at times caught small trout for the meals. A logger who worked with Dad shot a deer and gave us a hindquarter. This helped us to make it through the cold months. Because we were accustomed to hard times, we were able to survive. We had learned many times before what it was like to go without. There were no complaints, only a will to survive and hopes that living conditions would get better another day.

The weather finally warmed and spring came. I fished more and it seemed that fish were served at every meal. During late spring Dad taught us how to prepare the soil to plant a garden. We spent long hours breaking the soil with shovels and spades and weeding. We planted rows of vegetable seeds in the soil. When Dad explained that vegetables would grow from these seeds, Bernard became very interested. Every day he tended the garden, inspecting the growth of the plants and weeding when necessary. With my brother's help, I dug a narrow ditch that led from Manila Creek to irrigate the garden. Bernard was pleased to learn how to irrigate the plants, and he asked to be left in charge of that responsibility. He tended to the irrigation of the plants daily. Soon the growth of radishes, lettuce, peas, onions, and other vegetables appeared. Later carrots and potatoes grew in the soil. Bernard was very pleased.

Each day Bernard spent the morning on his hands and knees look-ing at the new plants as they grew. He was fascinated that the plant-ing of seeds could bring about other forms of life. Dad explained that vegetables would grow bigger and later in the summer we would have plenty to eat. Bernard was pleased that he was a part of what was hap-pening. He began to understand and appreciate the results of hard work.

During the first week of July 1943, Dad announced that he had de-cided to move us back near Inchelium, "I hear that a big logging com-pany is going to move into the Upper Hall Creek area. They are ex-pected to hire people to help with cutting trees and logging the timber. I think I might be able to get a job there. How would you children like it if we moved back home?"

The three of us were excited with the prospect. "We can visit Charlie and Eliza again," Bernard announced. "I haven't seen them for a long, long time. I hope they are taking good care of Goat. We'll be able to see our fish in the creek again. I bet they are bigger now."

Before returning home to Inchelium, Dad decided to introduce his youngest son to the big city of Spokane. He thought that Bernard would enjoy visiting a big city and seeing all that it had to offer. A few days later Dad tied a five-gallon water tank with a faucet on the left run-ning board. He fastened a small container of kerosene with a spout for our lamps to the rear of the right running board. Blankets and food for traveling were packed in the rear of the Model T. We left for Spokane that morning, again prepared for any event that might happen.

The sun was setting as we entered the city. Luana and I had already seen Spokane the year before, when we traveled from Chemawa and changed trains to go to Wilbur. Bernard was fascinated as Dad drove the streets of the city. He had never seen so many people. When it got darker the lights glittered on every street. Bernard felt he was in an-other world.

Dad drove into another section of the city. "I'm going to get a room at the Montana Hotel," he told us. "I have been there before and it doesn't cost too much."

He brought the Model T to a stop in front of a large building in the poor section of Spokane. People were entering and exiting. "This is where we will spend the night," Dad said. He told Brownie to stay and watch the car as we headed for the hotel.

Bernard was all eyes as he surveyed the building. He had never seen a building so big. "This is a hotel," Dad told us. "This is where people spend the night when they come to Spokane. We're going to sleep to-night in one of the rooms."

We climbed the stairs to find the room that faced a parking lot. Bernard was fascinated when he looked out the window. He enjoyed look-ing at the people and the cars below. Then his attention turned to the small room. Bernard looked in wonder at the sink. He could not be-lieve it when Dad showed us a toilet down the hall. Bernard had always thought that toilets belonged outside. After learning to flush the toi-let, Bernard could not resist doing it over and over again. He wondered where the water came from and where it went.

"You children wash up in that sink and get the dust off your hands and faces. I'm going to take you to a restaurant tonight."

"A restaurant? What's a restaurant, Dad?" Bernard asked.

"It's a place where people get something to eat. You tell the waitress what you want to eat and a cook makes it for you. They have tables where you sit and they serve you food. You don't have to wash the dishes after you eat. Someone else does that for you." Bernard was anx-ious to see such a place.

We followed Dad out of the hotel, walking in a tight pack together on the sidewalk. People looked at us curiously as we walked down the street. In return, Bernard studied them as they walked along. Some-times he looked back at them after they had passed. He was full of curiosity.

As we entered the restaurant, Bernard expressed wide-eyed interest in everything he saw. He had never seen so many people in one place. He eyed those sitting at the counter as they talked, smoked, or ate their meals. Bernard had never seen people eating at a counter. After we were seated in a booth, Dad ordered beef soup and glasses of milk for us. He had coffee.

"What kind of meat is in the soup?" Bernard asked.

"It's beef. It's cow's meat," replied Dad.

"It tastes good. It kind of tastes like deer meat," Bernard remarked.

He studied a piece of meat in his spoon. "Don't we get milk from cows? How can we get milk from cows if we make beef out of them?" He asked. Dad smiled and did not attempt to answer.

Bernard watched Luana wipe her mouth with a napkin. He copied her, not knowing why he was doing it. As we finished our milk, Dad walked up to the cashier and paid the bill.

"Why did you have to give that lady money, Dad?" Bernard asked.

"You have to pay for what you get, Son. Nothing is free."

Bernard thought a while and finally said, "That seems right. You have to pay someone if he gives you something. Nothing is free." Luana and I could see Bernard filing the words into some part of his memory.

After leaving the restaurant, Dad said he would like to show us the town. As we walked, we peered into the windows of the many stores. We had never seen so many things on display. Bernard had many questions about all they saw. Luana told Bernard, "You could buy a lot of things in Spokane if you had enough money."

"How much money do you think you would need to buy everything in those stores?" Bernard asked.

"It would have to be a lot. More than what we have," Luana answered.

Dad led everyone back to the parking lot. He had some bones and pieces of meat that he was given at the restaurant. Brownie wagged his tail as we approached. Dad gave Bernard the sack of food to feed Brownie. The dog crawled under the Model T with a bone in his mouth and chewed on it. We left the alley and were off to see Bernard's first movie.

We walked a few blocks to a movie theater. The marquee sparkled with many lights. Bernard could only stand and look. Dad said that a mystery about cops and gangsters was showing. We were excited and asked if we could watch it. Dad paid at the ticket window and bought each of us a sack of popcorn. This was a new experience for Bernard. He had never seen a movie before, and he had never eaten popcorn. Before the main feature there was a newsreel, mostly about the war, then a comedy showing Bugs Bunny. Bernard was entranced. He was completely absorbed after Elmer Fudd appeared on the screen. This would be a night to remember for him. He would never forget it.

I asked, "Did you like the movie, Bernard?"

"That was the best thing I ever saw. I really liked that Elmer Fudd. He is so funny. I hope we can see Elmer Fudd and Bugs Bunny again sometime. I wish we had a movie theater at Manila Creek. I could see Elmer Fudd and Bugs Bunny over and over again."

Bernard was still talking about the Bugs Bunny comedy as we entered another movie theater. This time we saw a Mickey Mouse comedy as Bernard sat, captivated. He was completely absorbed as he worked on his second sack of popcorn. The movie that followed was about cowboys and Indians fighting each other. Bernard and I were the only ones in the theater rooting for the Indians. When the Indians lost and were driven off by the cowboys, we left. Bernard and I were disappointed, "You should teach them how to shoot like you do, Lawney," Bernard advised. "The Indians should learn how to shoot better."

We walked back to the hotel. When we reached our room we washed our faces, brushed our teeth, and crawled into bed. We enjoyed the size and softness of the hotel beds. The mattresses were much softer than the wood planks and burlap bags in our house at Manila Creek.

The next day was a perfect July day in Spokane. The sky was blue and clear. It was warm and it promised to get warmer. After a breakfast of oatmeal and milk at the restaurant, we returned to the parking lot to feed Brownie leftovers.

"I have a surprise for all of you," Dad told us. "I am going to take you to the Natatorium Park. It's the biggest amusement park in the whole Inland Empire."

Natatorium Park was located alongside the Spokane River. It was a beautiful setting, and hundreds of people were already enjoying themselves as we arrived. There was a Ferris wheel, a merry-go-round, bumper cars, and several other rides that defied description. There were long rows of tents where we could see performances or try to win prizes. Hamburgers, hot dogs, French fries, ice cream, candy, popcorn, cotton candy and almost every drink imaginable were being sold. Bernard was overwhelmed.

Bernard tied Brownie to the Model T with enough slack in the rope to allow him to crawl under the car to lie in the shade. Dad gave us money to spend on whatever we liked. I went off by myself. Luana and

Bernard stayed close to Dad. As they walked to see the sights, Bernard was full of questions. Everything he saw was new to him. Dad took Bernard to a part of the park that had rides for small children. Bernard rode in a few of them while Dad and Luana watched, but then Bernard said he would like to just walk and look at things. Luana was content to do the same.

Later in the day the three walked up to a large tent. They were surprised to see me being forcefully escorted from the tent. Dad angrily asked the man why he was doing this.

"The people inside the tent don't like Japs. The boy had to leave."

"He's not a Jap. He's Indian," Dad argued.

I was bewildered as the man studied me. He finally remarked, "Well, I guess that's better than being a Jap." He walked back into the tent, closing the entrance flap behind him.

"Why did the man think you were a Jap, Lawney? Do you know what a Jap looks like?" Bernard asked with a confused look on his face.

"I don't know. All I know is we're at war with them and we're fighting them somewhere far away."

As the Model T passed Davenport an hour later, Bernard frowned. He was still at odds by what had happened. "We should try to find out why that man thought you were a Jap, Lawney. I wonder what a Jap looks like." Bernard thought a while, "Is a Jap like those people who dropped those bombs on those big boats, Dad? Are they the ones? The ones that the radio was talking about?"

"Yes, they are like the ones who did it. The Japs are really called Japanese and they live far away, across the Pacific Ocean, near the Philippines, where I grew up." Bernard seemed to be studying what Dad had told him. He remained quiet for most of the trip back to Manila Creek.

The sun was setting as the Model T pulled up to our house nestled in the pine and fir trees at Manila Creek. We were tired after a long and busy day. In the morning we would return home to Inchelium.

Befriending

School started a month after we moved to the Lincoln Lumber Company camp at Upper Hall Creek. We had a small cabin that bordered a pond full of eastern brook trout. Bernard had learned to fish that summer and caught his first fish there. On weekends we stayed at our house on Cobbs Creek, seven miles away. Bernard was disappointed to learn that the Halls had given his goat to friends who had a farm. The Halls told Dad they had more alfalfa to feed it. Bernard was satisfied after Dad explained that Goat would be better off there.

Bernard entered school in Inchelium with Luana and me that fall. His first day was a success. He made friends, liked the teacher, and enjoyed the class work. Bernard learned quickly at school. He confided to Dad that it was a good thing that Luana had prepared him for school. He was happy that he now had classmates his own age to play with him. He had much to tell Dad after the bus returned us to camp. He talked nonstop.

Thanksgiving came and passed, then Christmas. There was a lot of snow in the Inchelium area. We enjoyed the snow and spent a lot of time outdoors. Presents arrived a day before Christmas from Mom, who now lived in Tacoma, Washington. Bernard received a soldier's uniform of trousers, a shirt, and a coat. A metal helmet, World War I vintage, was in the bottom of the box. Bernard was delighted with Mom's gifts. I found a necktie in the package and tied it, as best I could, around Bernard's neck. He put the uniform on and admired himself.

Bernard in his soldier uniform with a Winchester rifle, Upper Hall Creek, Inchelium, Washington.

Everything fit very well. "Can I wear the uniform to school and show my friends, Dad?"

"I don't see why not," Dad replied.

"Can you take my picture while I'm in my uniform? With Brownie?" Bernard asked. Dad got his camera and they headed outside.

The next day Bernard wore the uniform to school. Everyone in his class surrounded him. They had never seen a soldier's uniform before, especially one that fit a small person. The boys took turns asking Bernard if they could try on his metal helmet. That day he was the center of attention and became even more popular with his classmates.

As spring arrived new grass and wildflowers appeared on the surrounding hills. Bernard and Luana played about the camp. Luana continued to tutor Bernard, who was beginning to read very well. After the weather warmed the two sat in the shade of the pines that bordered the pond. Luana read diligently as Bernard followed every line. If he didn't understand a word or the meaning of a sentence, he would always ask Luana what it meant. Bernard was always hungry for knowledge.

In May a letter arrived from Judge William C. Brown stating that the apple growers at the Jim Wade Orchards needed an interpreter, someone who spoke Spanish. The orchards were going to hire Mexicans to pick apples and none of them could speak English. Judge Brown knew that Dad was fluent in Spanish, and he reasoned that it would be a good-paying job for him. He advised Dad to be at the orchards by the end of August. Luana and I would have to go to school at Okanogan, and Bernard would go to grade school at a small town called Malott, about seven miles south.

Luana and I were concerned about moving to Okanogan. We knew the town was off of the reservation and that no Indians lived there. We were anxious about going to an all-white school. Luana and I remembered how white people had treated our family when Mom and Dad picked apples. We remembered the prejudice our family faced when white men continually harassed us. We wondered if we would face similar treatment when we went to school at Okanogan. Bernard did not remember the treatment. He was excited about the move. Bernard always looked forward to new places and new experiences.

At the end of June 1944, Dad purchased a 1929 Model A. The paint had faded on most of the car, and there were many rust spots. Dad suggested that Bernard and I paint the car. Bernard was excited when I told him that I would teach him how to paint. While Dad went to the general store to search for the supplies he needed, Bernard and I sanded the rust off the car. After Dad returned with cans of paint and brushes, Bernard and I went to work while Dad lit his pipe, relaxed, and sat down under a tree. Occasionally he gave Bernard advice on how to paint. Seven hours later the Model A was painted a bright kelly green, although much of the paint was on Bernard's shirt and pants. To our family it looked like a brand new car, and we were ready to travel to Okanogan.

We loaded everything we needed into the car. Dad bought an old trailer to carry everything else we would need. Luana, Bernard, and I were excited that the car had enough seats for everyone. Brownie would not ride on the front fender of the Model A. He wanted to ride in the back seat with Luana and Bernard. As we traveled, the three of us noticed that the Model A was more comfortable than the Model T. It traveled faster and took less than five hours to reach Okanogan.

Hundreds of acres of apple trees came into view as Dad drove the high plateau. This was the B & O (Boston and Okanogan) area, and the Jim Wade Orchards covered over five hundred acres of land. Dad would start work on September 1 as an interpreter. The orchards had hired about two hundred Mexican workers to pick apples, and Dad had been hired to interpret between the foremen and the Mexicans.

Our family's new home was two small concrete-block cabins. One would serve as a place for sleeping and the other for cooking, eating, and studying. The cabins had electricity but no running water. There were ten cabins in all, and a large building that had toilets, sinks, a place to launder clothing, and showers. Bernard was especially pleased. He had never experienced a shower. One could see his immense pleasure as the water splashed over him.

One of Dad's first purchases was a flat-topped heater. It was used to heat the cabin, and the top provided a cooking surface. Later he purchased a small electric heater that provided warmth in the second cabin where we slept.

A large warehouse nearby had been converted to house about one hundred Mexican workers. We found the Mexicans friendly, but it was difficult communicating because they could not speak English.

Every evening, after supper, the Mexicans brought out their guitars and played Mexican music. Dad played his guitar with them as we children listened and enjoyed the music. It was obvious that the Mexicans loved their music.

"Where did Dad learn to speak Mexican and play his guitar so good?" Bernard asked.

"I think it was in the Philippines, when he was young," I replied.

"He sure is good," Bernard said proudly.

Bernard entered school a week later in Malott, a small town about two and a half miles south of the Jim Wade Orchards. He was the only nonwhite in the school, but he was liked by his classmates and made friends easily. The schoolwork was much harder in Malott. Bernard had to spend hours after school studying to keep up with his classmates. Luana helped whenever Bernard had difficulties. I was also having problems keeping up with my classmates in Okanogan. The schoolwork was more advanced than the work in Inchelium. Luana was the only one who excelled at school. She caught on quickly to new material and had no problems with her studies.

One Saturday Bernard saw several army trucks arrive. They were filled with many tall young men. Many of them had blond hair. All of them were wearing uniforms that he had not seen before. Bernard walked closer and realized they were speaking in a language he could not understand. The men were guarded by a few American soldiers. Some of the men talked to Bernard in broken English, but he had difficulty understanding them. Bernard was curious and ran to get me. "Those men over there are talking strange," he told me. "One spoke to me but I could not understand him."

I studied them for a while. "I think those men are German soldiers, but I'm not sure. I don't know why they are here or how they got here."

"What is a German soldier?" Bernard asked.

"We're fighting them in the war just like we're fighting the Japanese. The Germans and the Japanese are on the same side, and we are fighting them." I studied them more closely. "Those men might be German prisoners. They were probably captured and brought here as prisoners of war."

Bernard was intrigued. "Where do the Germans live? Do they live close to the Japanese?"

"The Japanese live across the Pacific Ocean and the Germans live across the Atlantic Ocean, far apart from each other."

Later in the day Bernard and I watched as the German soldiers picked apples. I figured there were close to a hundred of them. One of the Germans walked up to us and started speaking English. He had a strong accent, and Bernard and I had difficulty understanding him at first. He had many questions, and we listened and answered as best we could. When the German learned that we were Indians, he was impressed and asked more questions that dealt with the Indian culture. The German asked about some tribes that I learned about when I was at Chemawa. I was surprised that the German knew so much about Indians. I wondered where and how he had learned so much of the Indian culture and ways.

Bernard became curious when the German talked about other Indian tribes. He had not thought about other Indians before. He was surprised that there were Indians who lived elsewhere. Bernard was even more surprised when I told him that many Indians spoke in a different language and followed different customs. Bernard had thought that the only people that lived in the world were white people, Lakes Indians, and the Japanese. Now he realized there were other people like the Mexicans, the Germans, and other Indian tribes. Bernard was intrigued at the thought of other Indian languages and ways.

Later Dad told us that the German soldiers lived only a few miles away in a prisoner-of-war camp. The Germans were at the orchards to help harvest the apples along with the Mexicans. Dad believed that the German prisoners were on work detail from a military base called Fort Lewis on the coast.

That fall Bernard and I talked to the Germans many times while they worked in the orchard. We learned to like them. They were polite and friendly. Bernard found it hard to believe they were actually the enemy and the United States was at war with them somewhere far away.

One night about a week before the apple harvest ended, a fire started in the large warehouse where the Mexicans lived. The fire had burned the electrical wiring and left the building without lights. Everyone inside was asleep when it happened. Luckily, someone awakened and warned everyone to evacuate the burning building. No one was hurt, but in their haste to get out most of the Mexicans lost everything. Nearly everyone lost the money they had made and stashed away to take home to Mexico to help support their families.

When daylight came Bernard and I followed Dad to the burned warehouse. We could see several Mexicans sitting outside wrapped in blankets. The fire had burned so fast that most of the Mexicans escaped wearing only underwear and the blankets that covered their beds. The three of us helped look for possessions that might have survived the fire. Bernard and I counted eight guitars that were burned beyond repair. Many of the Mexicans were in tears. They had lost a whole season's wages.

When the German soldiers arrived, one could see the deep concern they felt in their faces. They spent hours carefully combing through the ashes looking for coins and other items that might have survived the fire. When items were found, the Germans wiped them clean of the ashes and gave them to the Mexicans. It was a sad day for everyone there.

Bernard had been born into poverty and hard times, and by an early age the years of deprivation had toughened him. He never felt sorry for himself when he faced setbacks. But when he witnessed the sadness that had overwhelmed the Mexicans that day, as a seven-year-old, he felt the hurt deep within him. From that day on he would bear the distress of others personally. He would try his best to ease their burdens.

At the end of June 1945, Dad moved our family to the Malott Orchards, along the Okanogan River, about two miles east of the Jim Wade Orchards. These orchards were smaller, about one hundred fifty acres. That summer Luana and I would go to work with Dad, thinning apples. We had grown and could move the ladders now. That summer we would be paid for our work for the first time.

Bernard had met a few children his age and spent his time playing with them. During the day it was his job to bring cold water to us as we worked. The cabin we lived in was small, but because we had few belongings we adjusted.

In the summer of 1946 I purchased a King trumpet. When I was not thinning, spraying apple trees, or tending the garden we had planted, I studied lessons that were sent to me by mail from the American School of Music. I managed to learn the basics of reading music and could play simple songs.

Bernard was fascinated with the trumpet. "That trumpet is pretty. I'd like to learn how to play it, Lawney."

"You're very young, Bernard. But if you mean it, I'll try to teach you. Before you learn to play you have to know how to blow it. It's not easy." I picked up a sheet of music. "You have to be able to read this music, too. But that can be learned later. Do you think you can do it?"

"Let me try. Show me how you hold it. How do you make those sounds?" Bernard held the trumpet as I had. He put the mouthpiece to his lips and tried to blow. I explained how to pucker his lips and blow clear notes.

Weeks later Bernard had learned to play simple tunes. He did it from memory. I was surprised at how quickly Bernard progressed. By summer's end he had learned the basics of trumpet playing and reading music. A year later he was playing better than me. Bernard would eventually become the lead trumpet in the Okanogan High School band.

Our family lived and worked at the Malott Orchards until the end of July 1948. At this time Dad decided to invest in a house in Malott, a few miles south. With the help of Luana and I, now working in the orchards in the summer and fall, we felt it would be a good investment.

"How much do we have to pay for our own house?" Bernard asked.

"The owner wants seven hundred fifty dollars for that old house we looked at."

"That's a lot of money, Dad. Do we have that much?" Bernard asked.

"We don't right now, but in time if the payments are not too high we could pay a little every month until it's paid for."

The house sat on a quarter acre of land at the edge of Malott. Luana and I agreed we should put money down as soon as we could afford it. We all knew that if everyone worked together we could make the payments until it was our own.

The house had electricity but there was no running water. A water pump was located close by and an outhouse stood behind the house. It had two bedrooms. Luana used the larger bedroom while Bernard and I shared the smaller one that was barely big enough to hold the double bunk bed. Dad used the small living room as his bedroom and slept on the sofa that was left by the original owner. All of us felt good about owning a home of our own. To us it was an important accomplishment.

In May 1949, I graduated from Okanogan High School and went to work for the Great Northern Railroad. During the summer of 1950 I worked again for the railroad. I earned enough money to enter Wenatchee Junior College that fall. Luana graduated at the top of her class in 1951. Bernard was very proud of her when she showed him her diploma. A few days later she traveled to Tacoma to look for work and live with Mom.

In May 1951 I came home after finishing my first year at Wenatchee Junior College. I asked Bernard if he would like to go to Tacoma and stay with Mom and Luana. Bernard was excited about seeing them. He wondered if the large city she lived in was like Spokane. We left for Tacoma the next day. After hitching five different rides with strangers along the way, we reached Tacoma about eleven hours later.

As we traveled Bernard and I talked about Mom having married Harry Wong and now having three more children. Bernard asked if we were related to them. I told him that we were all one family now. After we arrived Mom introduced her three children, Junior, Teresa, and Laura. Junior was five years old, Teresa was four, and Laura was three.

At midday all seven of us got on the Portland Avenue bus and went to Harry Wong's restaurant for something to eat. Bernard and I enjoyed watching Harry play with and cater to his three children. After preparing a delicious lunch, Chester Wong, the number one chef, came from the kitchen to sit and visit with everyone as he enjoyed a cup of tea. During the summer Bernard and I visited often with Chester. He told us many stories of China and in particular, Canton, the city he came from. We became close to Chester.

That fall, Bernard entered junior high school at Okanogan and I returned to Wenatchee Junior College for my second year. It did not take Bernard long to adjust and make new friends. He enjoyed Okanogan, and his friends helped make his time there eventful. When he encountered difficulties in school, his classmates helped him and shared what knowledge they had with him.

During the summers Bernard worked in the apple orchards thinning and spraying the trees. After spending the day spraying DDT and lead, his clothes would be totally soaked with the pesticides. I had done the same when I was his age. No one knew the dangers of spraying apples with that type of mixture in those days.

During the fall each year the school closed for three weeks to allow the students time to work in the orchards. Bernard picked apples. He worked hard and shared what he made with Dad to help pay for food and other necessities. Bernard learned the value of money at an early age. He worked at whatever job was available so he could earn more. In the summer months I visited Dad and Bernard at our home in Malott.

Before his sophomore year in high school, Bernard got a job washing dishes at the Cariboo Inn Restaurant in Okanogan. It was a good job, and the cook grew to like Bernard. Every night after work he cooked a small steak for Bernard to enjoy. My brother had never eaten so well.

That summer Bernard managed to save enough money to buy his first car. He found an old 1934 Ford Coupe, and after some mechanical work and help from friends he managed to get it to run. The muffler was damaged, but Bernard never seemed to have enough money to repair it. He ignored the problem and drove his car—noise and all. Bernard was pleased with his new possession. This was the first time he was able to buy something for himself. He took friends for rides around Okanogan and Omak. He had to be careful and avoid the police, though, because he was not old enough to have a driver's license. When classes started in the fall Bernard drove his car to school, picking up friends along the way. When he could not afford gas for his car, he rode the bus with everyone else.

Several times, during the summers of those years, Dad and Bernard traveled to Owhi Lake, near Nespelem, or to Twin Lakes, further east, to fish. I remember doing the same when I was Bernard's age. Sometimes, Bernard invited friends who lived in Malott and Okanogan to go with them.

"If you guys are challenged about being non-Indian by the Indian Police, tell them that you are half-breeds," Dad advised. "They won't know the difference." When they reached Twin Lakes they pitched a tent at Rocky Point near the north end of North Twin. This was the only place on the lake where one could fish from the shore and catch the large rainbow trout.

During the summer Bernard and his friends sometimes drove to Green Lake for a day of swimming or to Omak Lake to go swimming in colder water. The lake was high up on the Colville Indian Reservation, and Bernard and his friends enjoyed the beautiful setting. During this time Bernard learned the mechanics of his car. He was soon able to make repairs whenever they were needed. Bernard enjoyed the challenges of repairing a car. It became a pastime that would last throughout his life.

In the summer of 1953 Bernard and his friends became interested in girls. Dances were held in Omak and Okanogan, and one night Bernard and a few friends went to the Sawdust Maker's Hall in Omak. Many high school students from towns nearby attended dances there, and a popular western band called The '49ers played there regularly. The Okanogan Valley Playboys, another local band, played at the Riverside Hall and the Brewster Open Air Pavilion. The big Saturday-night dances were held at Maple Hall on the flats above Okanogan and Omak. This was a large dance hall, and people from the entire Okanogan Valley came to dance to The '49ers music. Some came to drink, to visit, or just to fight later in the night. That summer Bernard and several of his friends learned to dance.

When the dances at Maple Hall ended, shortly after midnight, Bernard and his friends would race to their cars and drive to the Daisy Mae Drive-In north of Okanogan. They wanted to be the first in line to order hamburgers. Abner Wilson owned and operated the Daisy Mae and they served the greatest hamburgers in the Okanogan Valley.

When there was nothing else to do, Bernard and his friends hung out in The Den on Main Street. The Den had always been the principal hangout for students and alumni long before Bernard and his classmates used it. I had spent a lot of time there when I was in high school, six years before. Sooner or later everyone went there.

Dennis Key lived in Malott and was a friend of Bernard's. The Key family moved to Malott when Bernard was in elementary school, and the two became inseparable. They spent time exploring the area about the Okanogan River and went to the nearby lakes and streams to fish. Dennis and Bernard also explored the mountains together on both sides of the river. They loved the mountains and they experienced the beauty and all the wildlife that was a part of it. Dennis liked Bernard and was curious about Indians. He found the Indian culture fascinating.

One day Bernard invited Dennis to accompany him on a trip. He told Dennis that he would like to go to Wenatchee to visit a friend. Dennis said that he would go, but he had to ask his mother's permission first. After thinking about it for a short time, Dennis changed his mind and told Bernard that they should go right away but try to get back home before dark.

The trip to Wenatchee took nearly two hours. The damaged muffler of Bernard's car could be heard for miles away. This attracted unneeded attention as they drove through the small towns of Brewster, Chelan, and Entiat. The number of people walking the streets when they reached Wenatchee impressed them. The two had a great time driving the streets, sightseeing, and looking at the girls. They were always careful to avoid the police, though, because both were still too young to drive.

They did not get back to Malott until early the following morning when it was still dark. Dennis's mother was waiting for him. She was furious. Mrs. Key told Dennis that he was not to hang out with Bernard Reyes anymore. She said that Bernard was worthless, no good, and would never amount to anything.

During Bernard's years in high school in Okanogan, he was also close to Paul Schulz. They had met while both were in the ninth grade. Paul was tall and good looking, and he had a pleasant personality. Everyone liked him. Bernard and Paul spent a lot of time together enjoying what Okanogan had to offer. When he was a sophomore, Paul became an outstanding athlete and was exceptional in both football and basketball. When Okanogan played against their strongest opponents like Omak, Chelan, and Tonasket, Bernard was always there cheering for Paul. Bernard was always one of his best fans.

One day Paul asked his mother if he could use her house to throw a party for all of his friends. Paul knew his mother would agree to stay at a friend's place, allowing him the use of the house for the night. During the evening, while everyone was drinking beer and having a good time, Bernard walked about the house and marveled at its elegance. He had never seen a house so large and so nice. He had never seen polished oak floors. The large lounge chairs and sofa awed him. The fabric looked rich and expensive. He admired the luxurious drapery that covered the windows. The chandelier that hung from the ceiling in the dining area sparkled. The interior of the house had a pleasant aroma that matched the richness of the furnishings. Bernard was not accustomed to the feminine fragrance that lingered throughout the house. He thought it must come from the perfume worn by Paul's mother.

Bernard wondered what it would be like to have running water and indoor plumbing. He thought of the small windows at home that had no drapery. As he surveyed the stylish furnishings in front of him, he thought of his own home with its meager furniture. He could only shake his head and wonder. When Bernard told me of this I remembered the poverty our family suffered during our days in Okanogan. I could fully sympathize with Bernard's feelings when he walked through Paul's home.

The next day Paul's mother found out that her son had invited Bernard to stay overnight with the rest of his friends. She was infuriated. She told Paul they lived in the best neighborhood in Okanogan. She had no problems with Paul's white friends, but she asked her son what her neighbors would say when they learned that a "Siwash" was allowed to stay overnight in their home. Paul's mother said, in no uncertain terms, she did not want that "Siwash" in her home ever again.

Paul was shocked at his mother's anger. He did not understand why his mother was so upset. He left his mother's house and went to see his dad, who lived in a small home along the Okanogan River, a few miles south. Paul's mother had divorced his dad a few years earlier, and his father now lived in the small house by himself. His dad owned a small apple orchard and spent most of his time tending it. Sometimes Paul stayed with him.

Paul saw his dad working in the orchard and walked over to him. They talked a while then Paul asked his dad what a "Siwash" was. His dad wanted to know where he had heard that word. Paul explained that his mother had called Bernard that name earlier in the day.

His dad shook his head and showed his disappointment. He knew Bernard and liked him. He told his son that "Siwash" was a word used by white people who didn't like Indians. It was a word used to downgrade Indians, like "Nigger" was used to downgrade Negro people. When Paul heard that, he became shocked and angered. He could not understand why his mother would use a word so degrading on one of his best friends. Paul would never forget this encounter with his mother.

One afternoon as Bernard and his friends gathered at The Den, he was introduced to Pat Barnes. She became one of Bernard's favorite friends. She was a year younger, and he regarded her as one of the boys. She was a tall attractive brunette and full of mischief. Pat's family owned the local funeral home.

Bernard sometimes stretched the truth when talking to girls. Some evenings Pat and Bernard would sit in his '34 Ford Coupe and search for the answers to life's unanswerable questions. One night Bernard shared with Pat memories of his mother, Mary. She listened with an almost religious fervor. Bernard told her that his mother was beautiful and that she was an Indian princess. Pat, who knew nothing about Indians or their cultures, told Bernard that she thought that was so romantic. Pat did not know that, in reality, Bernard's knowledge of Indians had little depth, not much deeper than her own. Bernard did not know that either in 1953, when he was fifteen.

That year Bernard met one of Pat's classmates, Marilyn Hodgson. She was tall, blond, blue-eyed, and very attractive. Bernard was enthralled by Marilyn's appearance and freshness. He appreciated her directness, her honesty, and her intelligence. Bernard had never thought seriously about girls, but he fell for Marilyn the moment they met. Bernard, at first unsure of himself, invited her to go for rides in his '34 Ford Coupe. She went willingly.

Bernard took long rides with her about Okanogan and the Omak area. Sometimes they drove to Green Lake, above the flats, to join others who were swimming. Everyone could tell when Bernard and Marilyn were coming by the sound of Bernard's car in the distance. He ignored the problem and continued to drive the car whenever he could afford to buy gas.

Bernard and Marilyn went to movies together at the Avalon Theatre in Okanogan with other friends. Sometimes they drove to Omak, four miles away, and attended the theater there. They went to all the dances in the Okanogan area, joining others their age.

Marilyn's friendship was important to Bernard. It made him feel good about himself and helped him to see himself in a different light. Marilyn admired Bernard's feelings about life. He never let a day go by without taking full measure of it. He wanted to enjoy his friends and days totally because he was aware that time and life were precious. He wanted to live it to the fullest. Marilyn could see that Bernard was always positive in his thinking. He always tried to make each day a good one and this made her happy. I knew that the poverty in Bernard's life hurt him, but he managed to keep it hidden. He learned to set aside his problems and not allow setbacks to ruin his day.

Bernard soon began to spend most of his spare time with Marilyn. When Bernard drove Marilyn around he always showed her the utmost respect. When they arrived at their destination in his '34 Ford, he got out of the car to open the door for her. When the two entered buildings, he always made sure that he opened the door to allow her to enter first. Bernard's friends had never done this for their girlfriends, and they were amused to see Bernard scampering about doing this and that for Marilyn.

The first time Bernard returned Marilyn to her home after an outing, he was awed by the beauty and size of her house. It was a large, gracious two-story building with beautifully manicured landscaping. It sat majestically on a low hill surrounded by other homes of similar quality. To Bernard the house looked like a palace. It seemed to welcome visitors with open arms. It was obvious that this neighborhood was inhabited by people of means. As Marilyn left the car, Bernard studied the well-groomed entryway to her home. He could only sit in his car and wonder.

Marilyn's parents did not care for Bernard, but in the beginning they tolerated his presence. When they found that the relationship between the two had grown closer, they did their best to break them apart. They did not want their daughter in company with a person who was poor and nonwhite. They wanted someone better for her. Bernard was aware of this and knew he would never be welcome in Marilyn's home.

Bernard did not experience prejudice from his peers in high school. His friends were always good to him. It was the parents and other members of their generation that directed their prejudice toward Bernard. They regarded Indians as dirty, lazy, and shiftless. They were unaware or did not care about the hard times Indians were having in merely surviving a way of life enforced upon them. They did not know jobs were seldom available for Indians. When the owners of orchards could find no one else to do the work, they reluctantly hired Indians.

Bernard thought of this one evening as he drove Marilyn about the town of Okanogan. He could not fathom how or why this had happened to his people. It was disheartening for him to dwell on problems that seemed to have no answers. After they reached Marilyn's home, Bernard told Marilyn that he didn't think that he would be able to find a job in Okanogan now that he had graduated from high school. He might have to go to the coast to find work, perhaps somewhere in Seattle or Tacoma. They agreed not to worry about it, but it weighed heavily on Bernard's mind.

Bernard decided to travel to Tacoma. He stayed with Mom on Portland Avenue. He renewed his acquaintance with Junior, Teresa, and Laura, and when he was not looking for work he spent time with them. Often the four of them rode the Portland Avenue bus uptown to the city center of Tacoma and visited Harry Wong and Chester at the restaurant on Commerce Street. The four would enjoy the wonderful dishes prepared by Chester. Bernard thought that Chester was the best cook in the world.

Bernard soon found how hard it really was for an Indian to find employment. While he was there he searched for weeks hoping to find work. His efforts turned out to be fruitless. I was in the army and stationed in Germany at the time, and occasionally Bernard wrote letters and brought me up to date on what he was doing. I could tell that he was at loose ends during this period. He did not know which direction to take in his life. I could tell that his sense of self-worth was being questioned, probably for the first time in his life.

Searching

Bernard finally gave up his search for employment in western Washington and returned home to Okanogan. After some effort Dad was able to get him a job on the Okanogan section of the Great Northern Railroad. He was relieved to get the job during the summer because it allowed him to stay in Okanogan and be close to Marilyn. It was hot during the summer and the work was hard, but Bernard enjoyed it. He was able to earn enough money to enter the University of Washington in the fall of 1955.

The first year at the university was unimpressive for Bernard. Whenever he could afford it, he traveled to Okanogan to visit Marilyn. He did not devote the time required to achieve good grades, and he had no idea what field of study to pursue. His thoughts were always centered east of the mountains, with Marilyn.

Bernard remained at the university until the end of May. During the summer of 1956 jobs were still hard to find in Tacoma, but he was fortunate that he could live rent-free at Mom's home. Bernard became uncomfortable with thoughts that he had to rely on someone other than himself. He felt he had to earn money, and he decided he would not return to the university in the fall.

That summer Bernard met a man who would become very important in his life. The man was Bob Satiacum, a Puyallup Indian. Bob had dropped by Harry Wong's restaurant to get something to eat and visit our mother, Mary, who was waiting tables. Mom introduced Bernard to Bob. They talked a while and then decided to sit down. Bernard studied Bob closely. He was a good-looking man who stood about six feet tall. He had a medium bronze complexion with dark brown hair that covered his temples with natural waves. Bernard had heard of Bob. He was born in the Fife area near Tacoma and had lived there most of his life. Bernard knew that Bob had graduated from Lincoln High School in Tacoma in 1947 and that he was regarded the best overall athlete in the area. Bob excelled in football and basketball. Bernard liked Bob immediately and knew that this was a man he could respect and trust.

They agreed to meet at another time. Bob told Bernard that he usually came down to Pacific Avenue in the evenings to get some beer or eat at Harry's and he would take him to the "Indian taverns" the next time they met. He would introduce him to some of his friends on Pacific Avenue.

Bernard could not find work anywhere in Tacoma that summer. He spent days covering the tide flats and the Fife area. A few weeks later, he ran into Bob, who invited him to have a beer. While they were drinking at one of the Indian taverns, Bernard confided that he had been looking for a job but was unsuccessful in finding one.

Bob knew that jobs were hard to find around Tacoma, especially for Indians. That was why he was fishing in the Puyallup River for salmon. Runs were not heavy because it was too early in the summer, but that should change when it got colder in the fall. He invited Bernard to fish with him if he wanted to. He could lend Bernard a canoe with a motor and a net.

Bernard had never fished for salmon before. Only for trout, rainbow and eastern brook, with a pole.

Bob told Bernard he didn't use poles, only a drift net in the river. Bob ordered two more beers. Bernard noticed that Bob nearly finished a bottle every time he tipped it. He told Bernard that he could teach him everything he needed to know about drift-net fishing. The only thing that Bernard had to provide was guts for riding in an Indian canoe during windy nights on the Puyallup River and his own gas for the motor. Bob told him it would not be easy.

That afternoon Bernard went to Bob's house in Fife. The house looked like it belonged to the backyard. It was a small two-story dwelling with a gable roof. It had wood siding that was once painted white but was badly in need of a new coat of paint. There was a smell of fish everywhere. Several canoes and a few motorboats littered the backyard. A half dozen fishing nets, with cork floats, hung on the fence. There were motors for boats of various sizes propped against the fence. The canoes were narrow, carved from cedar logs, and about twenty to twenty-five feet long. Some had crude Salish and Northcoast Indian designs painted on the bow.

Bob told Bernard that he could use the white painted canoe with the small Mercury motor. The motor was simple to operate and reliable. Bob asked Bernard to give him a hand in placing the canoe onto a steel rack fastened to the bed of his pickup. He secured it with rope and hung a flag of red flannel on the end of the canoe. Bob removed a drift net from the fence, put it into the bed of the truck, and threw an orange life jacket onto the net.

Bob suggested that Bernard buy a pair of hip boots when he could afford them. A raincoat would come in handy, also. It would help Bernard to keep warm and dry when the weather got colder.

Bob advised it was necessary to have an inner tube with a secured lantern tied to the end of the net. This would help him know where the end of the net was when drifting down the river at night. Bob smiled as he told Bernard that it would also keep the police and the coast guard happy. He added that they were always looking for some excuse to give Indians tickets. Bob said he didn't think they liked Indians netting their fish. He suggested the whites believed they brought the salmon with them when they came across the Atlantic.

Bob drove his pickup through the tide flats to reach the mouth of the Puyallup River, where it flowed into Commencement Bay. Bob had fished the Puyallup since he was a young boy.

Bernard helped Bob unload the canoe. They placed it in the water and tied it with rope to a piling so it would not drift away. Bob attached the motor to the mounting bracket near the end of the canoe. He checked to see if the motor had enough gas.

Bob put the folded net into the middle of the canoe and the inner tube close to where he would be sitting. He gave Bernard some matches for lighting the lantern.

They seated themselves in the canoe with Bernard in the front and Bob in the rear near the motor. As Bob started the motor it gasped and sputtered. When it began to run evenly he steered the canoe upriver about a half mile.

Bernard watched how Bob laid out the net. He placed the inner tube into the water as the canoe pointed upriver. He slowly let out the net as the canoe made a half circle to point downriver. The position of the corks made a perfect bow in the river, and both the canoe and the net floated downriver with the current.

Bob said that if any fish came upriver they should hit the net. Bernard watched Bob's every move as they drifted to the mouth of the river. After the first drift Bob brought the canoe to shore and got out. He told Bernard to sit where he had and said that it was his turn to see if he could catch any fish.

Bob held the canoe steady and Bernard climbed over the net to sit in the rear. Bob sat in front. Bernard pointed the canoe upriver and slowed to set out the inner tube as Bob had done. He let it out in a half circle and drifted downriver. As they moved slowly down the river, they could see and hear the activity of people, seagulls, and cars in downtown Tacoma. Colorful neon lights sparkled everywhere.

As they drifted with the current, Bernard became aware of the unpleasant smell of Commencement Bay. The pulp mill to the west emitted odors that were offensive, and it carried into the Portland Avenue area where most of the Indians and people of low income lived. The smell of industry did not hamper the whites. They were fortunate. The winds carried the offensive odors to those who lived further east—to those who were less fortunate.

After a few drifts Bob turned to Bernard and said he didn't think there were any fish yet. The fish would start moving upriver in about a week. He suggested they go to Pacific Avenue to drink some beer, adding that they might get lucky and find some girls. Bernard was soon to learn that drinking beer and flirting with girls were two of Bob's favorite pastimes. Bob introduced him to every Indian in the three taverns on Pacific Avenue between 13th and 14th Streets. They drank beer, talked, and flirted with the girls the rest of the evening.

One night while they were drinking together, Bob told Bernard that he was low on cash. Bob said that he knew of a way to make some easy money. As they drove toward the outskirts of Tacoma, Bob told him that the fastest way to make a few bucks was at the slot machines. The taverns located outside of town, in the "boonies" as they were called, were the best places to go.

Bob confided his plan. Bernard was to play the jukebox continually to distract the bartender. While he was making a lot of noise, Bob would be playing a slot machine using his special technique. They would park his car about a hundred yards away. If he got caught they should both run like hell to the car to make a getaway.

As Bob played he drilled a small hole into the side of the machine and slipped a wire to trip the mechanism so that he did not have to use a coin. Eventually, the machine paid off. Bob made about ten to fifteen dollars, enough for hamburgers and more beer for one night. Bernard enjoyed the easy money and the adventure of it all.

At the end of August I returned from Europe. My tour of duty in the army was over. Mom and Bernard drove to North Fort Lewis to pick me up. As Bernard drove back to Tacoma, he asked me how I liked military life.

"I liked the army very much," I said. "They made me an offer. If I remained in the army one more year they would promote me to second lieutenant. After that first year they'd promote me to a first lieutenant. If I decided to make the army a career I'd be promoted based on my ability. I liked the offer and considered it. But after a lot of thinking I decided to come back and finish up my last two years at the university instead."

After dropping Mom and me off at her home, Bernard excused himself and left to visit friends. Mom prepared tea and offered me a cup.

"I'm glad we have time to ourselves," Mom said. "I want to talk to you about Bernard. Since you've been gone he's been spending a lot of time with a girlfriend from Okanogan. She went to school with him there. I think he's on his way to meet her right now. She came to visit a few days ago, and I'm concerned that their relationship is getting too serious." Mom sipped her tea quietly and thought. "The problem is she comes from a well-to-do family. I know her parents are against having their daughter associating with someone who is not white."

Mom reached for her pack of cigarettes, lit one, and offered one to me. "The girl is accustomed to a comfortable lifestyle that Bernard could never match. I think the problems they'd face would be greater than either could handle. I wish you would talk to him and share my feelings about this whole thing. Bernard has always listened to you, Lawney. He might take your advice."

The next day after Mom left for work, I found myself alone with Bernard. "Mom asked me to talk to you about your friend Marilyn." I sat on the sofa and lit a cigarette. "We both agree that you'll find it difficult to match the standard of living she's accustomed to. Her parents will never accept anyone who is not white into their family, Bernard. I hope you'll think about this very seriously." Bernard sat and listened quietly to everything I had to say. He did not speak a word.

The next day Bernard brought Marilyn to Mom's home. I was getting ready to register for the fall quarter at the University of Washington in Seattle. Bernard introduced me to Marilyn before I left. She was tall and very attractive. She seemed sincere and friendly, and I could understand why Bernard was attracted to her. I could not tell if Bernard had taken my concerns seriously. Marilyn was getting ready to leave for Pullman, where she would be attending her first year at Washington State College.

That fall Bernard spent much of his time with Bob Satiacum. Most of that time was spent on the Puyallup River in the canoe Bob had loaned him. The fish runs became heavier, and Bob and Bernard began to make money. They fished through the night. Bob's two brothers, Buddy and Junior, joined them. Bernard could see they were experts at this type of fishing.

On weekends I drove to Tacoma and spent time with Bob, his brothers, and Bernard. Sometimes I fished with them. When the fish were not running, the five of us sat in the dark, late into the night, in our canoes on Commencement Bay. As the waves of the bay rocked the canoes, we talked and smoked cigarettes. Sometimes Bob produced a bottle of bourbon and we took turns passing the bottle. It helped to supply warmth in the chill of the night.

Bernard and I were impressed with Bob and his brothers. They had a deep knowledge of the movements of salmon. It was as if centuries of knowledge had been passed down to the Puyallup Indians living today. They had an uncanny ability to sense when the salmon would make their runs up the river to spawn.

Since Kettle Falls on the Columbia River had been flooded over in the early forties, the knowledge of salmon and their behavior gradually slipped away from our people. Now there were only faint memories of the great salmon runs that only the elders could trace. We felt the Puyallups were fortunate they still had their salmon. We considered them rich compared to the people of our tribe, who were nearly destitute.

During the fall it rained continuously. When the weather turned stormy, gusts of wind blew sprays of icy water upon their faces. Bernard discovered that the taste of the water was salty. He had never experienced this before east of the mountains. The chill was different than the freezing cold back home. When the weather was bad the cold penetrated deep within, making it uncomfortable, but the rain gear they wore helped them withstand the elements.

Early in the morning buyers came to purchase the salmon that was caught. They were more than eager to buy the salmon because Bob kept the prices reasonable. The Indians not only needed the salmon for food but they needed the income just to survive from day to day. Fishing was hard, cold, and dangerous. Occasionally, one of the fishermen fell into the water. More than once the life jackets they wore saved them from drowning. Bernard fell in. He found it difficult to get back in the canoe once he fell because his hip boots would fill with water and add more weight. Luckily, the canoes only tipped. They were designed to right themselves and not roll over.

Bernard found that fishing for salmon with nets was hard work. Sand sharks had to be removed from the nets throughout the night. Jellyfish would become entangled in the nets, and it was difficult to remove them. The red jellyfish could sting painfully when touched. After a few weeks of strenuous fishing, Bernard noticed that his hands were covered with calluses. He felt that the muscles in his arms and back had gotten stronger and appeared larger.

They slept during the day in their cars, too tired to go home. When they were hungry, they went to the restaurants on the tide flats, where the staff ignored the fact that they were Indians. When the fish runs were not heavy Bob and Bernard spent their time in the Indian taverns on Pacific Avenue, where they drank beer and talked with the girls.

While they were fishing, the white sportsmen continually harassed Bob, his brothers, and Bernard. Most of the harassment came when they pulled the salmon from their nets in Commencement Bay. Almost all of the salmon they netted were on the Puyallup River, but when they drifted with the flow of the river to Commencement Bay, trouble came. Hundreds of white sportsmen fished Commencement Bay during the day in small boats. It angered them when they saw Indians removing salmon from their drift nets.

The harassment directed toward them usually took place during the day, when angry words were exchanged. More than once the white fishermen motored their boats over the drift nets trying to damage them. They wanted to make it difficult for the Indians to get their salmon. Bob, in turn, enjoyed taunting the whites.

One Saturday he pulled a forty-pound Chinook from his net and called out, "See this big fish. If you guys were better fishermen you would have caught it. But I beat you to it. I guess I'll take it home and have it for dinner." As he laughed over his comments, Bernard could see the rage in the faces of the white fishermen. Because of Bob's size, no one dared confront him physically. They could only sit in their little boats and fume.

At times whites came at night with designs to frighten the Indians. Bob carried a 12-gauge pump shotgun in his car in case trouble got serious. Sometimes he carried it in his canoe. Bernard did not own a gun, so he carried an axe handle in his canoe in case things got rough. During the night men who operated tugboats purposely entered the mouth of the Puyallup River and ran into the drift nets in an attempt to ruin them.

The coast guard would also interfere with the fishing at night. If lights were not on the canoes or on the inner tubes at the ends of the nets, the coast guard would give Bob, Bernard, and the others tickets that had to be paid. The coast guard was always looking for infractions they could enforce. It was simply a fight between whites and Indians for the salmon in Commencement Bay that were en route to the Puyallup River. Bernard found that Bob really enjoyed his adventures on the Puyallup River. He looked forward to the confrontations with the white sportsmen and the coast guard.

When the fish runs were not heavy, Bob, his wife, Myrt, and Bernard joined other Indians at the Old Mill just south of the town of Puyallup. The Old Mill was once a grange hall located in a forested area high up on a hill. The music was a combination of pop and country western. About three-fourths of the people who went there to dance were whites. The rest were Indians. Bernard noticed that the whites and Indians stayed with their own and did not mingle with one other. There was no courtesy and communication between the two groups. Inside, the whites and Indians seemed to cast blind eyes on each other. But sometimes in the parking lot outside there were fights between members of the two groups after they had drunk too much.

One night Bob, Bernard, and I sat watching the dancing. Bernard lit a cigarette and said, "I notice there is a lot of tension between the whites and the Indians here. Where I come from in Okanogan they don't have that problem. Differences don't seem that severe." Bernard drew on his cigarette. "Everyone seems to tolerate one another there. It's clear that the whites don't like Indians on this side of the mountains. About the only place Indians are welcome here is in the Indian taverns."

Bob flashed a knowing smile, "Where you come from Indians are probably not a threat to the whites. The white people have already taken everything of value from the Indians back there. Here the whites and the Indians are still competing and fighting. They are competing for the salmon," Bob said. "The whites here know that what's valuable is the salmon. They feel the salmon is theirs and they are not willing to share them with anyone. The white commercial fishermen don't like Indians getting in the way of big profits. The white sportsmen look at salmon as their sport. Sometimes I think they are worse than the Washington authorities. To Indians, fishing for salmon is not a sport. It is survival." I listened with interest as the conversation continued.

"I'm amazed at how ignorant the whites are about treaty rights," Bernard shared. "They seem to live only in their own little world, ignorant about the needs and rights of others. They have created a playing field that is not level and passed laws to sustain it. The laws are always created in their favor. The problem is they ignore those laws and they don't abide by them. Treaties and laws, they reason, are made for others. The whites break those treaties and laws whenever it becomes an obstacle to their greed. I have never witnessed so much greed in any one people. I wonder what kind of God they believe in. What kind of God would allow those that believe in Him to treat others so badly?"

Bob nodded his head. "Bernard, out on the water you've experienced the whites trying to intimidate us. They are always trying to force us to stop fishing. They are continually trying to damage our nets. Sometimes it gets pretty rough. To hell with them! I'm going to get in their way for as long as I'm here. As far as I'm concerned, the whites are fighting a losing battle. The law will admit one day, when the judicial system becomes honest, that we are right."

Bernard had thought of this before. He could see the truth in Bob's reasoning, and he had to agree with Bob's forecast of the future. Through Bob's eyes, Bernard could see clearly the big picture in western Washington. He understood the difficulties that Indians would face until something happened that would favor either the whites or the Indians.

Bernard thought that fishing with nets was a difficult way to survive, but he realized the Indians who lived in the area had something to strive for. This was something the Indians east of the mountains did not have. During the fall the silvers, then the Chinook, and finally the sockeye came in good numbers. The fish are what the Indians needed to survive. This is what they needed to fight for. He realized that the Indians back home really had nothing left but the reservation. The reservation was land set aside for Indians, it was a gift from the white man. In truth, it was land that the whites had no interest in. Bernard realized that he was now part of a challenge with another purpose, for Indians to catch their share of salmon that was rightfully theirs. I was impressed with Bernard's ability to observe and qualify complex issues. During those days I could see his thoughts growing and forming.

As we talked I noticed that Bob never seemed to show any emotion when he was concerned or angry. I could only see in the darkness of his eyes his true feelings. At those times they seemed to grow rock hard. When Bob was in good spirits he grinned and his eyes sparkled. At those times he looked like a big teddy bear. Bob was never a man to lie, but he did exaggerate the truth when he wanted to aggravate deceitful white men. When he related those stories later among his friends, he was full of laughter.

It was during this time that Bernard developed a taste for salmon. He grew to favor the salmon over the rainbow trout he used to eat back home. Bob taught Bernard how to prepare the salmon—how to cut the salmon down the front to remove the insides, the backbone and all the bones connected to it, then split it in half. Bob showed him how to fasten the salmon to cedar stakes that were driven into the ground and placed in a circle around a strong hot alder fire to give the salmon a unique flavor. When they were found, Bob roasted salmon eggs in an oven. The roasted eggs had a fishy flavor that did not appeal to Bernard, but he grew to yearn for the Indian-style baked salmon. The taste made me remember how much I used to like salmon back home before the completion of the Grand Coulee Dam.

In the summer of 1957 Bernard decided to make a change in his life. It bothered him when he realized that he had to depend on his mother and Harry Wong for lodging and food. He wanted to find a way to support himself. He was destitute and needed money, and fishing provided an income for only a few months of the year. Bernard was interested in seeing new places. That September he enlisted in the U.S. Army.

Bernard was curious to see if he could make it in the 101st Airborne. He was sent to Fort Ord in California to take his basic training. Then he went to Fort Campbell in Kentucky to become a paratrooper in the 101st Airborne. It was tough duty, but Bernard enjoyed the daily challenges that he faced. When the time came to parachute from an airplane during maneuvers, Bernard grew to enjoy the jumps. He always carried his camera and took pictures of his buddies as they floated down in their parachutes.

He made many friends during his days there. His buddies appreciated his sense of humor and his easy-going nature. Many of them had never met an Indian before, and at first they were curious about him. As time went on they became the best of friends. While Bernard was training at Fort Campbell his thoughts always drifted back to the Indians in Tacoma. He thought of Bob Satiacum and the difficulties he and his brothers faced in just trying to survive from day to day.

Occasionally Bernard wrote letters to Mom, keeping her informed on how he was doing at Fort Campbell. In one letter he wrote that after heavy training, he and his friend Bob Perry and three others went to Nashville, Tennessee. They spent the day walking about and taking in the sights. As night came on they heard music, and the five came to a large dance hall with many people entering. The music sounded good. Bob Perry suggested they go inside. Each paid their admission and walked in. But when Bernard tried to follow, a bouncer stopped him at the door. The bouncer announced loudly that no Mexicans were allowed in. Bernard was surprised and explained that he was not a Mexican. He told the bouncer that he was an Indian. The bouncer laughed loudly and informed Bernard that was worse yet. One day Mom let Bob and I read Bernard's letter. I thought it was funny. Bob just shook his head.

Bernard went on to write that his buddies were outraged and they wanted to tear the place apart, but he quieted them and said he would take a walk around the city and meet them later.

Later Bernard and his buddies met at a tavern and drank beer. They were still angry at how he had been treated. One offered to go and kick the hell out of the bouncer, but Bernard told him to forget it. Everyone had the right to his likes and dislikes, Bernard thought, and he had that right and everyone in the room had that right. People didn't have to like each other. It was not that important. Bernard told everyone in the tavern that he really didn't like anyone there and that was his business. He ordered one of his buddies to get him a beer and pay for it. Everyone laughed, and they spent the next two hours drinking.

During Bernard's tour of duty in the 101st he became a Green Beret. Bernard enjoyed the intensive training, and he liked the buddies he trained with. They were all good men. Bernard felt good that he was able to pass the intensive tests of becoming a Green Beret. He considered reenlisting when his tour was up, but then he thought about the Indians in Tacoma and believed he could somehow make their lives better by fighting for Indian rights.

After his tour in the service ended in 1959, he returned to Tacoma. He stayed with Mom on Portland Avenue. At that time he learned that Boeing had landed an important contract and was in the process of hiring. Bernard applied for a job and within days he was working at Plant Two in Seattle, fabricating parts for the jets. Bernard liked the job and enjoyed the income, but his heart was still with the plight of the Indians.

That summer Bernard joined an Army Reserve Special Forces team (Green Beret), in South Tacoma. The team's commander was Mike Layton. Bernard became the weapons specialist. During the summers the team spent two weeks of annual training in the Wasatch Mountains in Utah. Mike and Bernard became good friends.

Months later Bernard decided to change his name. He wanted to honor his grandfather, White Grizzly Bear. He shortened White Grizzly Bear to Whitebear so it would fit on a nametag while he continued to work at Boeing. He also shortened Bernard to Bernie. He grew to like the new name "Bernie Whitebear" and thought it a good and fitting name.

While in Tacoma he renewed his acquaintance with Bob Satiacum. Bernie remembered the efforts of white sportsmen to take from Indians what was rightfully theirs. These rights were agreed upon long ago, but the white sportsmen ignored these laws and harassed Indians daily during the fishing season.

Later Bernie met other Indians from western Washington, the Nisqually and Muckleshoot. These tribes were also having trouble with Washington authorities and the sportsmen. They were poor, and they needed the salmon they caught to simply survive. Bernie found that the relationship between whites and Indians had grown worse while he was gone. It was always difficult for Indians to find jobs. These men needed the salmon to feed their families. The white sportsmen and state officials harassed them as they fished their river. Several violent confrontations occurred. People on both sides were injured and bloodied as they fought in boats and on the shores of the river.

Billy Frank Jr., Al and Maiselle Bridges and family, Janet McCloud, and others in the Nisqually tribe fought for the Indian fishing rights at Frank's Landing on the Nisqually River. The confrontations were calculated to break the Indians' will to continue. Equipment, such as boats and fishing nets, were confiscated several times by the state.

Bernie and other Indians in Seattle were angered by the treatment of the Nisqually on their river by the state authorities. When a coalition of white sportsmen joined the state officials, bitter fighting occurred on the river.

The Indians in Seattle knew that the Nisqually were right. Treaties made long ago allowed them to take their share of salmon. Knowing that the Indians were outnumbered, Bernie and several friends from Seattle joined the Nisqually at Frank's Landing to give support. Bernie, ever the prankster, could not resist changing his attire. He adjusted a leather headband low around his head, barely allowing his eyes to show. He removed his pants and put on a self-made breechcloth that showed his muscular but slightly bowed legs. He could not find any moccasins to fit him so he wore an old pair of white sneakers that had holes about the toes. He found a bamboo pole about six feet long to which he tied a white chicken feather.

Afterward, I was given a blow-by-blow account of the incident. The Nisqually and their supporters had not met Bernie. They were curious to know who he was and where he came from. Bernie received the attention of everyone there as he stood holding his bamboo pole.

Janet McCloud walked up and asked, "Who are you? What is your name?"

Bernie answered, "My name is Buffalo Chips." Janet, a bit confused, managed a guarded smile.

A Nisqually asked, "What are you carrying in your hand?"

Bernie looked at the bamboo pole and studied it. He turned to the Nisqually and said in all seriousness, "I think this is a bamboo pole with a white chicken feather tied to it."

When the Nisqually realized Bernie was playing with them, they all laughed. After that Bernie made many friends in the Nisqually tribe. They never forgot that short Indian in a sagging breechcloth carrying a bamboo pole with a white chicken feather tied to it. They never forgot that he came down from the great city of Seattle to bring cigarettes, food, and containers of hot coffee. They remembered that Bernie was always there to lend support at Frank's Landing in their time of need. I heard of Bernie's exploits several times while I lived in Seattle. I smiled as I thought of Bernie's unique humor as he devoted himself to helping his people.

Marlon Brando and Bob Satiacum fishing for salmon in the Puyallup River, Tacoma, Washington, 1964. *Courtesy Seattle Times*

Later, Bernie traveled with Bob Satiacum and fished in the Columbia River near Portland and Astoria, Oregon. Bob wanted to test the Washington officials. He wanted to see where the state would actually enforce their rulings against Indian fishing. As they traveled and fished, Bob shared much of his knowledge with Bernie. He exposed his feelings about what and where he thought Indians could win against Washington.

During June 1964, Marlon Brando came to support the Puyallup and Nisqually tribes. While he was in Tacoma, he listened to Bob and Bernie as they shared the Indians' problems with him. He learned of the injustice the tribes were facing. Later, he spoke on behalf of the Indians who were being harassed by the state officials and the sportsmen. I saw a photograph in the Seattle *Times* of Marlon Brando speaking to a large audience in Olympia, Washington. Behind Brando, Bob and Bernie stood in finely made war bonnets. As I studied the photograph, I saw Mom standing in the audience. She was always there to show her support.

It was important to have men of Brando's stature speak for the Indians because they had the ability to sway those who did not recognize and understand the Indian's legitimacy and cause. The presence of Brando attracted the media. The newspapers and television stations were always present when Brando appeared. They were not really interested in Indian issues or Indian treaty rights but they were ever present when a big star like Brando was present. Marlon Brando actually fished with Bob and other Indians and was escorted to the police station, but the authorities refused to arrest him. The police did not want to risk bad press by jailing a popular and well-known celebrity.

Marlon Brando encouraged Peter and Jane Fonda and Dick Gregory to come and lend support. The big names helped the Indians to get favorable media coverage. In addition to his continued support, Brando gave money to Indians in need. Later, he actually gave forty acres of land that he owned in California back to the Indians. He apologized for being four hundred years late in returning that land. In 1972 he stated forcefully in *Newsweek*: "Christ Almighty, look at what we did in the name of 'democracy' to the American Indian. We just excised them from the human race. We had four hundred treaties with the Indians and we broke every one of them."

During those years Bernie met others in Tacoma, along the coast, and in eastern Washington who eventually became his friends, Indians from the Puyallup, Muckleshoot, Quinault, Nisqually, Yakima, Spokane, Couer d'Alene, and Duwamish tribes. All were in some way dedicated to fighting for their rights and improving the quality of life for Indian people.

Fishing with Bob Satiacum and his involvement with the tribes in western Washington took all of Bernie's time. He rarely had time for recreation or rest. He thought of Marilyn often during that time and he missed her. He realized how close and dear she was to him, but he remembered my words, "You'll never be able to give her the kind of life that she has been raised to accept and appreciate." Bernie could not dispute this reasoning. He wrote Marilyn at Washington State College, telling her he thought it best they go their separate ways. Bernie made it clear he would never forget her. He confided that he would always have good thoughts and strong feelings for her, but he had to find his own way and so did she.

From time to time Bernie would run into friends from Okanogan, and it would bring back memories of his time there. For the most part they were fond memories, and he would never forget them. Bernie missed the close friendships he had with his classmates.

He also ran into people from the reservation where we once lived. He had many questions and he asked about the welfare of friends he once knew. Bernie was also curious about the politics of the reservation and what was being done to improve the living conditions there. Bernie missed the beauty and the climate of eastern Washington. He missed the seasons, the hot summers and the dry cold of winter. Bernard felt out of touch with the lifestyle of his people and the quiet beauty of the mountains and forests. But he knew that those days were over and that his future would hold a new way of life.

Bernie realized there was a great difference in how white people and Indians thought. Their philosophies about life and the environment in which they lived were far apart. Bernie did not understand this when he was in Okanogan. He became aware of it after meeting coastal tribes like the Puyallup, Nisqually, Muckleshoot, and Quinault, who were at odds with white authority. The central issue for all of these tribes was the salmon. The whites believed all salmon were theirs. Whites were adamant that they did not have to share the salmon with any Indians, regardless of laws or treaties. In defiance to these laws and treaties, they continually broke the law as they tried to break the will of the Indians.

Bernie knew the Indians were right and that they had no recourse but to fight for their rights. Bernie was angered when he saw a video of the Nisqually fighting with the Washington authorities and the white sportsmen. He could barely contain himself when he witnessed the bloody faces of both Nisqually men and women defending their right to fish on the banks of the Nisqually River. Several of them were his friends. It was a matter of survival and tradition.

One night Bernie and I took the Portland Avenue bus to Pacific Avenue in downtown Tacoma. We wanted to have a drink and enjoy the evening. Bernie wanted to talk with someone to pass the time. He asked the bartender at one of the Indian taverns, "Have you seen Bob Satiacum? Has he been around?"

"I haven't seen him for a few days. I hear he's traveling around the state looking for trouble," the bartender said as he flashed a perceptive smile. "He'll probably show up soon. Bob is always looking for new places to net salmon. He knows that is what white sportsmen don't like, and he can't help but antagonize them whenever he can."

While we were drinking three friends, George Meachem, Robert Taylor, and Gary Kalapis, came in and joined us. George was a Warm Springs from his father's side and a Swinomish from his mother's. Robert was a Yakima transplanted from the Yakima Indian Reservation. Everyone knew Robert as "Chief." He was a large man who weighed over two hundred pounds. Chief had worked as a longshoreman on the docks in Tacoma and loaded hundred-pound sacks of grain and cement daily since he was sixteen years old. He had developed a powerful body and loved confrontations. Chief was a rough fighter who could take a person out with either hand, and he could usually finish the job with one punch. When Chief was not fighting, he enjoyed drinking and telling his favorite jokes to anyone who would listen. Some thought Chief was a joke himself, but no one had the courage to tell him that to his face. Gary was of Polish descent and he lived in the Portland Avenue area. He had been friends with George since they were little.

The five of us moved to a booth and ordered more beer. "How did you like being in the 101st, Bernie?" George asked.

"It was good duty but very rough. Took me a while to get used to jumping out of planes. I thought more than once about making it a career and re-upping before my tour of duty was over, but I finally changed my mind."

Bernie tipped his bottle and took a long drink of beer. "I felt that more important things needed tending here at home. I don't know at this time what that could be, but I'm thinking about it."

"I thought of joining the 101st Airborne once, but when I looked at myself in the mirror I realized I was just too heavy," George shared. "I think I'll try the Marines."

Chief scoffed as he lit a cigarette. "I wouldn't waste my time in any service. I like my free time. Besides, it would take away from my time with the girls. And my drinking," Chief added.

"Just stick to drinking," George finally suggested. "You're too ugly to be thinking about girls."

During this time Bernie and his friends spent a lot of time together partying and drinking. When they had enough money, they went up to Harry Wong's to get some Chinese food. Yet, in their rowdiness they shared intimate information that revealed the hardships they each faced daily. They always supported each other in times of need. They soon formed a fraternal order to bolster their spirits. They called themselves the "Skins." The members liked to compare themselves to the Elks, the Moose, and the Shriners, the fraternal organizations of the white man. They claimed to have three lodges where they held their meetings, the three Indian taverns between 13th and 14th Streets on Pacific Avenue. If they could not be found in one lodge, they would probably be in one of the others.

"Sometimes, when we're all together we don't have time for Indians in real need because we are so busy attending to the multitudes of problems that face them. God help us," Gary joked in slurred words brought on by too much drinking. Gary tipped his bottle of beer and finished it in one gulp. He yelled to the bartender to bring him another. I watched him in amusement. I realized the hopelessness of his comments. It was obvious he was more concerned about having a good time than worrying about the plight of Indians, but he was a good friend and everyone liked him.

When the Skins gathered, others gave them a wide berth. If anyone had the audacity or courage to stand up against them, fights broke out, and the opposition soon learned that it was best to avoid any confrontations with anyone associated with the Chief.

One night at one of the Indian taverns, the Skins were discussing the events of the last few days. I was sitting at the bar by myself. There was too much noise at the tables where the Skins sat, and I preferred to be alone. But I could not help hearing what they were saying. "Do you have as much trouble as me in getting a job?" George complained. "The only place I can get a job is in the berry fields at Puyallup. Imagine a great warrior like me picking raspberries."

"If you were white, like me," Gary countered, "you wouldn't have any trouble at all."

"You're not white, you're a Polack. And that isn't much better than a Skin," Chief retorted. Gary ignored him. He tipped his bottle, finished it, and called the bartender for another.

Later Chief advised George, in all seriousness, that he was scheduled to visit his doctor and have an artificial eye inserted. He had lost his eye in a fight months before and had been wearing a patch. His friends were so accustomed to seeing him with the patch covering his wounded eye that they began to call him "Chief One Eye." He told everyone that night, "I'm having a hard time deciding what color the artificial eye should be." George mumbled incoherently from too much drinking, then advised, "Why don't you get a red one. It will match your other one."

As the night wore on their talking and drinking were interrupted only when good-looking girls entered to join the crowd. All the Skins would watch every move of the girls until they were seated. Knowing the reputation of the Skins, the young women would seat themselves as far away from them as possible.

Occasionally, Zola Kipp would come in. All discussion stopped, and all eyes followed her as she walked by. Everyone in the Indian community recognized Zola as the most beautiful girl in the world. I had seen her a few times when I came to get something to drink and talk with those I knew. I had to agree that Zola was indeed a knockout. She was a Nez Perce with a stunning figure who needed no make-up. She was the idol of every man in the community, Indian or white. Zola was a pleasant distraction to the Skins. Over time, they had developed a mundane existence, and most of their conversations revealed it. This was especially true when they had been drinking. When Zola was around their thoughts centered on more uplifting things. She was like a sliver of light during a very dark night.

After she had passed by, Chief ground out a cigarette on the table-top and toasted her with his bottle of beer. He stood and bowed. He declared to his friends, "When I finish this beer I'm going over to Zola and ask her if she would like to go out and have a good time with a real man."

Bernie laughed, "I wouldn't waste my time if I were you." He finished his beer and burped. "You're not in her class. Besides that, she's a fox. I really think I'd better do it."

"Both of you are dreaming," George pointed out. "She wouldn't give either one of you the time of day. If you're lucky you might stumble on her when you're tepee creeping. But after she saw how ugly you were, that would be the end of it."

Bernie began to realize that at the root of the Skins' humor was a serious problem that needed tending. They spent most of their time drinking, talking, and trying to solve all the world's needs. Bernie knew that this was only a shallow exercise in passing time. It was during this period with the Skins that Bernie began to think that he should be doing something more worthwhile with his life, but he did not know then exactly what that would be. Bernie felt he was destined to do something important in life.

During Bernie's talks with the Skins, he listened and became aware of the many problems they faced each day. They did not complain and would mask the hardships with carefree dialogue and heavy drinking. Eventually, the talks revealed their innermost struggles. At times Bernie would witness the intense anger of his friends. Fights would break out. This, he knew, was the result of the frustration they all faced because of the prejudice directed toward them by white people. This was fueled by the lack of recognition of the plight of Indians by the city and state governments.

Bernie did not know then that this anger would be the force that would later unite all Indians to follow him in his quest for land in Seattle. He had learned much of Indian problems in his conversations with his friends, but he felt it was time to move on with his life, to somehow help relieve the problems of his people instead of just talking about them.

I enjoyed hearing of the Skins many exploits. I thought they were funny, but I also realized that Bernie was learning much about the problems of urban Indians and would soon find ways to help them somehow.

Bernie could see that more Indians were moving into Seattle and Tacoma. They were coming in not only from reservations in Washington but also from other states as far east as the Great Plains. Indians were leaving their homelands and settling in urban areas because they were having trouble surviving on their reservations. There was nothing left for them there. For Indians to survive, they had to find work in the cities.

Many were aware that their plight was due to the U.S. government's policies, which began in the 1950s, regarding termination and relocation of Indians from their reservations. The government encouraged Indians to give up their land in exchange for money and move to the cities to start new lives. Most Indians were aware that a change of location and lifestyle would be difficult, but they really had no choice. They had been born and raised on reservations, and it was the only life they knew. It was hard for them to know that they would have to leave the quiet peaceful life of their homes for an unknown environment of concrete, bricks, and steel.

In the cities Indians found themselves isolated and struggling in their own little world, far away from their traditional homelands. This was due to an apparition of Manifest Destiny that the white man was still pursuing, leaving no room or consideration for Indians.

Bernie understood that these were not the best of times for Indian people. They were facing new problems as they tried to cope with the living conditions of the urban areas. The Indians that left their reservations soon learned that the Bureau of Indian Affairs and the Indian Health Services had developed a policy that in effect meant "once you leave the reservation, you are no longer Indian." The Bureau of Indian Affairs and Indian Health Services restricted their services to Indians who still resided on or near reservations and were under the administrative authority and jurisdiction of tribal governments. This troubled Bernie very much.

Bernie was aware this was a ploy designed by the federal government to move Indian people off their ancestral lands and into the mainstream of society. It became known as the "termination era." The federal government had planned relocation programs to move thousands of Indians into cities with promises of better employment and educational opportunities. Once the Indians were in the cities, there was no help to be found.

Indians learned that this was an attempt to terminate the tribe's trust status with the federal government and liquidate all tribal assets. This would be the final injustice to Indian people by the federal government after reducing total Indian land to fifty-five million acres and presiding over the decimation of Indian culture and religion. The grand planners of the Eisenhower administration saw this as the coup de grace in separation of Indian people from their last vestiges as a distinct race of people.

Now that Indians were stranded in cities, when someone became ill there was never enough money to pay for medicine or a doctor's care. Some Indian children had a poor attendance record at school and fell behind because of illness. Many had bad teeth because neither young nor old could afford to go to a dentist. There were no places to go for recreation except for the Indian taverns on Pacific Avenue.

The largest group of Indians in the Tacoma area was the Puyallup Tribe. Some of these people were friends of mine. They had a land base but they did not have enough money or expertise to do anything with it. The young were becoming self-conscious and sometimes ashamed because they did not have good clothes. Many wore patched hand-me-down clothing. Most wore ill-fitting shoes, and some had no shoes at all. Because of this, Indians did not venture into the nicer parts of town. They could not afford the merchandise in those areas, and they looked and felt out of place. They felt more at home with their own kind in the poorer sections of town.

Bernie could see that the overall culture was suffering because there were no facilities for Indians. There was no capital to cover the costs of creating facilities.

One Saturday Bernie came upon a pow wow near Portland Avenue. Pow wows were festive events usually celebrated by Plateau or Plains Indians. They served as an important place to display drumming, singing, and dancing. Usually competitions were held to see who was the best in a variety of traditional dances. Since many of the Indians had moved from their reservations to urban areas, this was an important way of maintaining ties with others of their tribe.

I was already there at the pow wow talking to Bob Satiacum. Bernie watched and noticed that the dancers and drummers were trying to emulate Plains-style songs and dances. He realized the participants were mostly Coast Indians but they were beginning to set aside their traditional ways of singing and dancing. They were beginning to adopt, however poorly, the Plains and Plateau styles.

Bernie did not accept what he was seeing. He thought it was a mistake for tribes to relinquish the unique qualities of their own cultures. Bernie felt if this continued, the tribes would forget the important things that made their cultures unique. He thought this could be the beginning of the end for the tribes in western Washington.

As Bernie's mind searched for answers to the problems he and his friends faced, his thoughts shifted to the problems that Indians faced in the past. He became angry every time he thought of how our own tribe, the Sin-Aikst, was dispossessed of their land, their culture, and finally their well-being. He could barely stomach how much was lost.

The final blow to our tribe had been when they were relieved of their original name, Sin-Aikst, by Congress in 1872 and renamed the Lakes. This came after they were stripped of their land and forced to become a part of the Colville Confederated Tribes on a much-reduced parcel of land. Everything of value was taken. The dispossession was so complete that the newly named Lakes inherited little more than the wind. Bernie vowed that he would do all he could to make sure the Indians who now lived in Tacoma and Seattle, those who had been forced to the cities to survive, would somehow fare better and retain what little was left of their cultures.

When Bernie thought of how Indians were portrayed in the movies, in novels, and passed over in the U.S. history books, he mused at the make-believe world created by the white man. He was amazed at the U.S. government, who professed the United States was founded on principles of democracy and freedom for all.

One night as Bob and I sat with him in one of the Indian taverns, Bernie vowed to change the image forged by the dominant culture. He pledged that he would dedicate his life to focusing the blind eyes of the U.S. government on the poverty, hardships, and needs of the Indian people living in urban areas. Bernie was determined to do this to rectify what he considered a criminal act against his people. I told Bernie that I thought he was facing an extraordinary challenge, one that certainly would take his entire life to accomplish.

There did not seem to be any answers to the problems he was beginning to observe. Bernie realized then that things would not change for the better unless something unique happened, something eventful. He vowed that he would make that happen, somehow.

Another Warpath

In 1966 Bernie decided to move to Seattle. Most of the Indians he would be dealing with lived there, and he wanted to be closer to his work at Boeing. He rented an apartment on Beacon Hill. Since my family lived close by, I saw Bernie often. From time to time we got together in the International District at a favorite watering hole and discussed the problems that Indians were facing.

Bernie felt his first priority would be to tend to the young people of the tribes. As the Indian population grew, the city was becoming a magnet that attracted Indians from different parts of the country. They would have to be coached on how to adjust to living in an urban area. The Indian youth would have to learn to balance their lives, to straddle cultures. It would be important to retain what they knew of their cultures and then learn more about it. At the same time, the young would have to learn the complexities of the white culture. Bernie felt this would have to be accomplished if the young Indians were to prosper in an urban environment.

While in Seattle Bernie spent much of his spare time organizing so the young could learn Indian singing, drumming, and dancing. He requested the aid of several Indians knowledgeable in the drumming and singing of the Plateau and the Plains. Sometimes I would go and watch. Many young people were anxious to take part in learning the traditional songs and dances of their respective tribes. This encouraged Bernie, and he devoted more time to organizing singing and dancing groups. As he worked with them, Bernie learned to sing over a dozen well-known songs of the various Plateau and Plains cultures.

Bernie organized and threw his first pow wow at the Masonic Temple in Seattle in 1961. It was a huge success. I was impressed with the quality of the performers' dancing. I especially enjoyed watching a hoop dancer who performed at the end of the pow wow. Bernie was somewhat surprised but pleased that many white people appeared in the audience. It was clear they enjoyed the performances of the Indian participants. Because of the success of this first venture, he was encouraged to throw more and larger pow wows.

In the summer of 1961 Bernie went to a Colville Indian meeting in Seattle. He unexpectedly found Mom, Luana, and my family there. The meeting had been organized to discuss the merits of termination of the Colville Indian Reservation. There were about one hundred fifty people there, all members of the Colville Tribe. Most of them lived in and about the Seattle area. Bernard noticed that many were half-breeds who could pass as white. As the meeting went on several people spoke, giving their opinions of termination. Most of the people there seemed to prefer termination when it was revealed that the U.S. government would give each tribal member sixty thousand dollars. This was a conditional offer to any Colville member who would approve termination and give up their rights as American Indians. The reservation was covered with good stands of timber and minerals that could be of worth in the future. The government wanted to make the land available to logging companies and mining interests.

Bernie could see the danger of termination to Indians, especially to those Indians who still lived on the reservation. He could see the attraction of receiving sixty thousand dollars for those who lived off the reservation and had few ties to their homeland. It was a lot of money for those who had always had little. But the Colville Tribe voted unanimously to keep the reservation. Bernie was pleased that his tribe had the foresight to do this. The reservation provided little wealth to the members of the tribe, but at least it was theirs to own.

Bernie became uncomfortable when he thought of how the business of the tribe was conducted by the tribal council in Nespelem. He kept track of the policies and happenings of the Colville Tribe by reading the Colville *Tribune*, a monthly newspaper of the tribe that was printed in Nespelem. It became obvious that the twelve council members spent more time fighting among themselves than working together to improve the living conditions of the people.

Over the years this was a continuing problem. It seemed to Bernie that the first order of business for every council member was to guarantee that each of his or her constituents would get a per capita check. Council members seemed convinced that this promise to their constituents would ensure that they would be reelected for another term in office. Bernie wondered how long the Colville Tribe could last under this type of leadership.

The Colville Indian Reservation was created by executive order of the president of the United States in 1872. Bernie was well aware that if greedy forces wished, the president would be forced to return the reservation to the overall public domain. Bernie knew that anything that Indians owned was at risk in this country. He was uncomfortable in knowing that Indians could lose everything if white people deemed it profitable to acquire it.

Bernie was disappointed when he learned that whites owned some of the best parts of the reservation. The members of the tribe could own land in two different ways. Most had trust land that was managed by the tribe. If a member wanted to sell trust land, it could only be sold to another tribal member. When the land was in trust status, taxes did not have to be paid. But if members so desired, the land could be put in patent-in-fee status and they were free to sell the land. But the member would also be required to pay taxes on the land to the county seat. It became clear to Bernie that the policy of granting Indians patent-in-fee allotments was disastrous. Because there was little employment on the reservation, Indians found it hard to make money. When taxes were due it was impossible for Indians to pay them. Eventually, they were forced to sell their land. Since most Indians had no money, the only ones who could afford to buy land were white people. Bernie regarded this practice, known as "checker boarding," as another ploy used by the U.S. government to take land from Indians.

Bernie was convinced that Indians who came from reservations must retain ownership of their lands. He knew it was the only thing they had that was of value. Bernie knew that many would be forced to move from their reservations to find work to support their families in other areas. But, regardless of where they lived, they would always be Indians and a part of the lands they came from.

Bernie knew that all Indians in the cities would have to straddle cultures to survive. They would have to understand white ways and adjust to them. He knew it would be hard to live in two cultures, but if Indians were to succeed, they would have to make a strong effort to do this. Indians would have a difficult time because they would be a minority living within a majority who could not care less about Indian cultures and traditions. Bernie knew he must find ways for Indians to retain the cultures that were a strong part of them. This would present a great challenge for him, but he would find a way to do it. I realized that Bernie's struggles would be difficult, but I could tell he was determined to do this for his people.

During the mid-1960s it became apparent that Bernie was a born entertainer in his own right. He joined a group at Boeing that performed musicals. The musical "Annie Get Your Gun" was ideal for Bernie. He played Sitting Bull. He had never appeared on the stage before, but he became the star of the show. In one scene Bernie had to carry a passed-out Annie across the stage. During the evening performance, the young woman playing Annie was petite, and everything worked out fine. But during the matinee, Annie was played by a tall woman, actually much taller than Bernard. When Bernard struggled to carry her across the stage, one hand dragged along the stage floor. The audience broke into uncontrollable laughter.

Everyone enjoyed Bernie's performance as Sitting Bull. Several members of the audience came from Tacoma to see the show. Malcolm McCloud, an attorney who was a friend of Bernie, liked his portrayal of Sitting Bull so much that he came and sat through three performances.

In 1968 the Koleda Dance Ensemble, a Balkan folk dance troupe, invited Bernie to travel with them if he could assemble a Native American dance group. They were scheduled to travel throughout Europe on a three-month tour. Bernie was able to bring several of his friends together. Somehow they raised enough money to sustain themselves during their trip. They flew to Europe with the Koleda Dance Ensemble and were scheduled to perform in Greece, Turkey, and other countries close by. Later, they would go to western Europe and perform in Germany and France. I was amazed that Bernie was able to come up with the money for this trip. I knew those Indians who went with Bernie would consider it a journey of a lifetime.

Bernie loved to relate the experiences of that European trip to anyone who would listen. He invited a white friend of his, Moose from Tacoma, to come along. Moose was a giant of a man. He weighed two hundred and sixty pounds and was over six foot eight inches tall. Moose helped on the tour in a variety of ways. He carried the equipment, drums, and other regalia for the dancers and was available to anyone in need.

Before one of the performances a few of the drummers and singers caught a cold and could not sing. Bernie realized that the show could not go on without them. It was too late to cancel. He asked Moose if he would pinch-hit and sit at the drum.

"Hell, Bernie I can't do that stuff," Moose wailed. "I wouldn't know what to do."

"You're going to have to fake it, Moose. I don't think the audience will know the difference," Bernie promised.

Moose put on the reservation hat that Bernie gave him. The eagle feather in the headband distracted from his overly short braids, hastily put together by one of the girl dancers. He took a drumstick and stared critically into a mirror, "My God, I look stupid in this getup, Bernie."

"I don't think you look that bad, Moose, but I admit I have never, ever seen an Indian quite like you before."

"Tell me about it, Bernie," Moose sighed.

Moose looked a bit out of place as he sat at the drum, towering over the other drummers, but he tried his best at singing some of the Indian songs. It turned out alright, though, as the audience concentrated on the dancing.

While on the tour, Bernie noticed that when the Indians were just walking through the streets of the cities, they were ignored. But when they appeared in their costumes Bernie and his troupe became the center of attention. Hundreds of people surrounded them, wanting to look at them, touch them, and take their photographs. During their performances the press was always there wanting interviews. Europeans were very curious about American Indians. Like the German prisoners we had met as children, many knew more about Indians than white Americans. They understood the problems Indians were having in their own land and the plight they were experiencing in trying to adjust and survive with what was left of their world. Bernie realized Europeans respected Indians and held them in high esteem. That was something missing in the white world of the United States.

These experiences in Europe helped Bernie realize his calling in life. Bernie knew that several of the tribes who moved from their homes on reservations to the cities were once ancient enemies. Those tribes would have to forget their animosities. He felt that the various tribes would have to forge a united front to cope with the federal, state, and municipal policies that were directed against them.

When Bernie realized his destiny, he was anxious to return home and begin his work. His first efforts would be to make Indians more visible to white people. He would do this by throwing pow wows, large ones. Bernie invited the best singers, dancers, and drummers from the Plateau and Plains tribes, but he also made sure that the songs and traditional dances of the Coast tribes were represented at the pow wows. He knew that many whites in Seattle had never seen this type of entertainment. He felt, in time, they would come to see and experience pow wows firsthand. This would be his first step in educating white people about Indians and their cultures, the first step in trying to gain respect for his people. Bernie was determined to make Indians visible and respected. This had never been done before.

In 1968 the first large pow wows were held in the Arena at Seattle Center. These events were much larger than the one he threw at the Masonic Temple. I was surprised to see how many participants came and how many tribes were represented. The costumes were beautiful. Although the pow wows were large and colorful, Bernie realized that something was missing. It did not seem natural to him that the dances should be held indoors on polished wood floors. They should be performed outside, closer to nature.

At this time Bernie became aware that the Indians in Seattle had no place of their own. There was no setting for large numbers of Indians to gather, to practice and enjoy their cultures. Bernie knew that one of his first efforts would be to change this. He would have to find a place for Indians, a place they could call their own, a place where they could gather in the hundreds, share their culture with friends, and be themselves. But in the late 1960s there were no avenues open to approach this goal.

Bernie also became acutely aware that thousands of Indians had no medical services available to them. The Indians had come from different reservations, from different parts of the country, to find a way of survival in Seattle. All were poor and could not afford the services of doctors, dentists, or medical clinics. Bernie knew that he would have to find a way to change this soon or the plans of survival in the cities would fail.

Bernie and I met often to discuss these matters. He used me as a sounding board for the ideas that flowed through his mind. There were many times when I had no solutions to problems, but that never seemed to stop him. His mind was full of ideas and always operating at top speed.

In October 1968 I received a telephone call from a woman who was sobbing uncontrollably. I had difficulty understanding her. After she calmed down a bit, she told me that my dad's house was on fire and they could not rescue him. I realized she was a neighbor. I gathered my family together as quickly as I could, and within hours we arrived at Malott. Our dad's body had already been removed. It was dark and there was a chill in the air. We stood quietly in front of the house that was half burned, remembering the days when we lived there. We remembered our dad's loyalty and how hard he worked over the years to guide and support us.

We realized as we stood there that we actually knew little of our father's history. Dad did not talk of his past. We knew he came from a little town near Manila. Dad had never gone to school. He taught himself the English language and how to read. After that he taught himself to write, eventually developing a beautiful penmanship. We did not know if Dad had any relatives in the Philippines. The only thing that seemed important to him was that he loved the Colville Indian Reservation and all the nature that was a part of it. He was also very proud of his three children, Luana, Bernard, and me.

No one knew for sure what caused the fire or why Dad was unable to get out. The funeral was held on a cold October day. A dozen friends of our family came to pay their last respects. All were old and some were not in the best of health. It was comforting to see these old friends and one-time neighbors again.

Later, we went to the Cariboo Inn in Okanogan to stay the night. Bernie and I spent a part of the evening alone in the lounge having a drink and reminiscing about our high school days. He spoke of Marilyn, wondering where she was and how her life had turned out. He remembered the days when he had worked in the restaurant at the Cariboo washing dishes, the friendship that had developed with the cook, and the delicious steaks that he prepared for him.

In the morning our family returned to Seattle. We stopped one last time to view what was left of our home and retrieve what we could. As we walked through the ashes, we found that everything of value had burned. Only a silver-coated crucifix survived. Bernie picked it up and wiped some burned and blackened remains from it. He remembered seeing it for the first time in our little house at Cobb's Creek when he was very young.

After we returned to Seattle, Bernie continued to work with young Indians, teaching them a variety of Indian songs and drumming. He also worked with adults from various Plateau and Plains tribes who knew the dances of their tribes. Bernie began to learn the unique qualities of the many songs and dances. While Bernie was doing this, he also devoted his thoughts to getting land in the city and healthcare for the Indians who now lived there.

In 1969 Bob Lupson, an Alaskan Native and a member of Kinatchitapi, an urban Indian organization in Seattle, learned that Indian children in Seattle were missing school because of sickness. There were no hospitals that offered low-cost care. Bob felt that free clinics were needed to provide badly needed healthcare.

Bob and several other volunteers started a free clinic for Indian people at the U.S. Public Health Service Hospital. Lyle Griffith, a member of the Oglala Sioux Tribe, was in residency training at the University of

Washington Hospital. He and his wife, Donna, became involved and were soon organizing volunteers to staff a more comprehensive free clinic.

The number of doctors who volunteered grew to thirty. Later, Peter and Hinda Schnurman, recently arrived from New York City, joined them in 1970. They volunteered their time to work and find funding. They were instrumental in setting up the free clinic. Peter and Hinda drafted the first funding grant. Peter also spearheaded the development of a volunteer dental clinic. Later, the actual incorporation of the Seattle Indian Health Board took place in the Schnurman's living room. Donna Griffith took the incorporation papers to Olympia the next day.

Soon afterward, Jill Marsden joined them. She had recently moved to Seattle from England. She had expertise in management and grant writing, and she took charge of the planning and development of health services. Eveline Takahashi, a pharmacist, joined Jill. She organized a volunteer pharmacy to administer to those who were sick and in need. The six worked together closely and spent much time as volunteers gathering the resources and organizing the new free clinic. I was very much impressed and appreciative that non-Indians would devote so much time to the needs of people of another race.

Dr. Willard Johnson, the director of the U.S. Public Health Service Hospital in Seattle, was contacted. Dr. Johnson was sympathetic to the needs of the Indians. He made available clinic space at the hospital so that volunteer doctors, nurses, and other health professionals could administer medical and dental care to sick and impoverished Indians.

Bernie knew the problems they faced were enormous, and he contributed as much time and effort as he could. It was at this time that he left Boeing. He did not have energy and time to continue his work there and attend to Indian needs at the same time.

Lyle Griffith became the first medical director of the Seattle Indian Health Board in 1969, and a year later he became the president of the board of directors. When the first funding was obtained, Lyle and Peter realized they needed a powerful spokesperson who was a member of a local tribe. They knew Bernie was a great speaker and asked if he would be willing to apply for the position of executive director. It would be

Jill Marsden, Seattle,
Washington. *Courtesy
Jill Marsden*

Dr. Lyle and Donna
Griffith. *Courtesy Lyle
and Donna Griffith*

Bernie Whitebear, Jane Fonda, Bob Satiacum, and others at a news conference in Seattle, 1970. *Courtesy Seattle Post-Intelligencer*

important to have a director who would always be there to lead the new health organization they were proposing.

Bernie became the first executive director of the Seattle Indian Health Board. Later more funds were obtained, and Bernie had enough money to hire Jill Marsden as his assistant director. Jill became the chief administrator of the organization. Within days Jill and Bernie were sharing all responsibilities of running the organization. Not long afterward, they had enough funds to hire a secretary, Roberta Middleton. From that time on, the three were working long hours, sometimes well into the night.

The formation of the Seattle Indian Health Board was the first major achievement for the Indian community in Seattle. The Seattle Indian Health Board grew from the dedication and inspiration of six important volunteers, and in time it would help thousands.

Bernie was pleased with his part in establishing a medical facility to care for Indians. He was selected as the executive director because he was Indian and well spoken. He admitted he actually knew little about healthcare, but he did his best while holding the position. He depended heavily on Jill Marsden's expertise to handle the growing burden of administrative challenges, and Bernie was fully aware of the contributions made by Jill. He knew that he could not have made the advances necessary without her involvement and help.

Bernie served as executive director for about a year. But the need to acquire a land base for Indians became uppermost in Bernie's mind, and he resigned his position. Jill Marsden ran the Seattle Indian Health Board until a new director was selected.

The Seattle Indian Health Board advertised nationally and selected Luana Reyes to replace her brother as the new executive director. Luana had lived in San Francisco for nine years. She had returned to Washington at the end of 1962 and worked for a large accounting firm in Seattle, Northwest Administrators. Luana loved her job there, but she wanted to get involved with Indians. She wanted a job where she might be able to contribute something important to help her people. Luana would learn of Jill's expertise, as she worked to build the organization during the next ten years. During Luana's tenure as the director of the Seattle Indian Health Board, the staff grew to nearly two hundred and it became a role model throughout the nation. People would say later that Bernie planted the Seattle Indian Health Board, but Luana grew it. I was proud of their involvement with the organization. It made me feel good that they were able to make it what it was.

Under Luana's direction the Seattle Indian Health Board became a multimillion dollar operation. It was, and still is, the largest and most successful organization of its kind in the United States. The organization became the first to receive a doctor, dentist, and nurse from the National Health Service Corps. During those years Hinda Schnurman joined Luana as the assistant director and ably helped her in the administration of the organization.

But Indians still needed a land base they could call their own. Bernie's understanding of this occupied most of his thinking. This dream of acquiring land was always on his mind. The reality of this seemed distant until February 1970, when Bernie learned that, with the reduction of services at Fort Lawton, the city of Seattle would be in line to get any land that was relinquished. Bernie reasoned that land could become available to Indians, and rightfully so. He realized this was what he had been waiting for. He, along with others, knew this would be the way of getting the land they needed.

Bernie held meetings with other Indians to determine whom they would approach to request land. I attended most of these meetings to show my support.

"The time has come for us to take action," Bernie stated forcefully. "A portion of Fort Lawton is closing. Land will become available to the city. I understand they are going to try to get about six hundred acres. We need to organize because I want some of that land. I want that land for our people."

"How do we go about doing that, Bernie?" Bob Satiacum called out from the back of the tavern. "How much land are we talking about?"

"As much as we can get, Bob."

"Bernie, we need to get the support of every tribe in this state," Joe DeLaCruz advised. "Out of respect, we should keep the tribes informed of any decisions we make in regard to getting this land."

Bernie nodded in agreement. He knew of Joe's knowledge of tribes and how much he was respected by them. Bernie liked and respected Joe, who was nearly his age. He accepted Joe as a part of the family because he was married to our cousin Dorothy Lemery from the Inchelium area. It was common knowledge by many Indians across the nation that Joe DeLaCruz had a thorough, in-depth knowledge of probably every Indian tribe in North America. Bernie also knew of Joe's importance to his own people as the director of the Quinault Tribe and how Joe had fought vigorously for self-governance for his tribe.

"Right now, I need people that are able to help me organize."

Several volunteers came forward. One asked, "What's our first order of business here? Who do we deal with? These are questions we must answer before we go any further." Bernie reached for a pack of cigarettes. He lit one and advised, "That's why we're here. We'll determine that tonight."

I found the meetings interesting as I sat and listened. I was beginning to witness Bernie's innate leadership qualities. They seemed to grow as the demands grew. I began to wonder where it would all end.

As time went on more and more meetings were being held, sometimes two and three a day. Each meeting seemed to attract more activists. Some were non-Indian. At one of these meetings, it was determined a request for the land would be made directly to the mayor of Seattle. They would arrange a meeting with Mayor Wes Uhlman.

Initial attempts to sit down and present their requests proved fruitless. Bernie Whitebear and the Indians who followed him were unable to reach agreement with the mayor's office. The city felt that the Indians should channel their issues through the Bureau of Indian Affairs. Wes Uhlman and his aides felt it was important that the Indians go through the proper channels. The city felt that the present Indian Center, located in an old abandoned church off Stewart Street in downtown Seattle, was adequate to accommodate the needs of Indians.

The Magnolia Community Club, representing the interests of the Magnolia and Lawton Wood communities, considered the land to be released by the army at Fort Lawton their own. Many of the residents of Magnolia were wealthy. They wanted to use the land as their own personal park. When they learned that Indians were also after this land, it made them uncomfortable. They did not feel it necessary to share what they considered to be their land with a group of Indians who were barely surviving in the city of Seattle. They began meeting regularly with city officials in an effort to influence decisions in their favor. The Magnolia Community Club would use their political clout and money to get this done.

Realizing that the Indians were having difficulty getting their messages to the mayor's office, Bernie decided to get help from important Indian organizations across the country. Within days young Indians from all over the United States came to Bernie's aid in his quest to get land. Various Indian leaders, selected by Bernie, met and planned the strategy to make Indian needs known. The formation of the plan began to take place, the plan to invade Fort Lawton. Others accepted the strategy Bernie put forth in the Indian taverns about Seattle.

Bernie assigned responsibilities to various leaders he could depend on. Everyone agreed when Bernie suggested that Fort Lawton be invaded from two different points. One party of about one hundred would scale the cliffs at the west end of Fort Lawton. At the same time three hundred would go over the fences at the north end of the fort near the Lawton Wood community. They agreed that the takeover of the fort would be nonviolent. Before the invasion, Bernie called his assigned leaders together for one last meeting.

"When we invade the fort we will surely meet resistance," Bernie announced. "It may get rough. I want you all to hold your temper, in spite of the difficulty and pain you might face. If any of you need alcohol or drugs to get you through this, forget it." Bernie spoke with conviction. "I don't want to make the same mistakes that were made at Alcatraz. I want to win this one." As I sat listening, I saw again that Bernie was truly a leader. I trusted his convictions, and I had a feeling that he would accomplish what he believed in.

At first light on March 8, 1970, hundreds of Indians went over the fences as planned and a tepee was set up to designate a command post. Others scaled the cliffs to the west. The military police were the first to witness a dozen Indians setting up a tepee that symbolized the occupation of the fort. They were caught by surprise, and help was requested from Fort Lewis. Armed troops arrived and squads of Seattle police officers were sent to help the army round up the Indian invaders. At times tempers were lost and fighting broke out. The leaders Bernie had selected had to intervene more than once to maintain order. The Indians that were caught were put in the stockade. Some escaped, only to return later in the day accompanied by new arrivals. Outside the main gate of Fort Lawton, five hundred Indians and non-Indian allies assembled to show their support to the invading activists. The media was there with their cameras.

When the army released Bernie Whitebear from the stockade, he announced in front of the press and television cameras, "We, the Native Americans, reclaim the land known as Fort Lawton in the name of all American Indians by right of discovery."

The invasion of Fort Lawton made national and worldwide news. Television and radio stations and newspapers covered the events. Additional coverage was given when Jane Fonda came to Seattle to give support to Bernie's efforts. The press was delighted when Grace Thorpe, the daughter of the great athlete Jim Thorpe, arrived. Cameramen had

Bernie Whitebear with Wes Uhlman and Joyce Reyes, Pioneer Square, Seattle. *Courtesy Seattle Times*

a field day when they took pictures of four military policemen strug-gling to carry Grace to the stockade. She weighed close to three hun-dred pounds and smiled as the MPs valiantly tried to move her. Indi-ans and their supporters everywhere remained glued to their television sets, surprised and fascinated by what was happening in Seattle.

I found the invasion of Fort Lawton awe-inspiring that day. It was obvious that the hundreds behind Bernie were determined to follow his lead regardless of the outcome. I knew that his large army of volun-teers would follow him wherever he went. To me, it was heartwarming to see so many young Indians pledging their loyalty to my brother.

Because the city continued to refuse to meet with the activists, Ber-nie sought legal advice from two prominent Indian attorneys in Seattle,

Bernie Whitebear being escorted to the stockade by two MPs during the invasion of Fort Lawton. Bob Satiacum is at left talking to another MP and George Meachem is in the center in a dark shirt. *Courtesy Seattle Post-Intelligencer*

Grace Thorpe, daughter of the great Olympic athlete Jim Thorpe, waits for the MPs to take her away to the stockade. *Courtesy Seattle Post-Intelligencer*

Gary Bass and Blair Paul. The attorneys advised him to form an organization that would be recognized by all as the body that would represent the Indians in Seattle. Within days Bernie and his staff created a name for their newfound organization, the United Indians of All Tribes Foundation (UIATF). Bernie was elected the first executive director.

Not all Indians in Seattle agreed with Bernie's leadership and methods in dealing with the city. At least four wanted to lead the Indians in their quest for land. In the beginning Bob Satiacum felt he should be the leader of the invasion, but it soon became evident that Bernie had by far the most followers. Others who did not agree with Bernie's plan of action stepped aside when they realized his following was too great. Pearl Warren, the founder of the American Indian Women's Service League, did not agree with Bernie. She was satisfied with the modest funding granted by the city and did not want to jeopardize it. She felt that forcing issues would reflect badly on the league.

Bernie, on the other hand, felt that the needs of Indians in Seattle would never be considered by the city without the use of force. The Indians in Seattle had never been demanding and always settled for whatever the city officials deemed adequate. Bernie knew that the numbers of Indians had grown in Seattle and now represented many tribes. It was time they demanded greater consideration. All Indian organizations had to stick together and be of one mind. They had to be united. To determine who would lead the Indians, from that point on, a vote was taken. Bernie won overwhelmingly.

Meetings were held with Pearl Warren, but she could not be persuaded to change her mind and support Bernie and the UIATF. It became obvious that Pearl would have to be replaced. Her term of office was nearly up and she was due to run for reelection.

At a UIATF meeting it was decided to run Joyce Reyes against Pearl. Joyce was the first who suggested that Fort Lawton be raided, and she knew the Indians in Seattle could no longer deal with the city officials as they had in the past. Because of greater needs in the Indian community, she felt they had to be more demanding, more forceful.

The present membership of the American Indian Women's Service League had always backed Pearl, and it was expected that they would do the same at the next election. The membership had to be increased to get new votes. New Indians would have to be brought in from the tribes that had moved into Seattle, and soon many were.

The UIATF did not foster any ill will toward Pearl Warren, but they felt a new president of the American Indian Women's Service League was necessary to unite all Indians in Seattle. All of the Indians who grew up in Seattle and were around before the influx of the new Indians from the reservations appreciated the formation of the American Indian Women's Service League by Pearl. All considered Pearl Warren a fine person dedicated to the needs of Indians in Seattle. Pearl was the first in Seattle to form an Indian organization that benefited the needs of Indian people who lived there.

But the majority of the Indians now in Seattle were aware that it was important that the city face a united front, so they could not pit one Indian organization against another. At the league's election Joyce Reyes won by a large margin. Now they could present a strong united Indian front to demand their needs. I was convinced that Bernie had formed a force to be reckoned with. At this time the Indian population in Seattle was about twelve thousand. I knew they would support Bernie if he needed their help. It seemed to me that Bernie would eventually win this important battle.

Later, Mayor Wes Uhlman and Senator Henry "Scoop" Jackson held a press conference concerning the Fort Lawton property. They promised the Seattle community that it could look forward to the city receiving the land for its exclusive use as a city park. No mention was made of the interest or desires of the Indian community to participate in Seattle's future plans for the property. The city's first order of business was to get the land for its own use.

Bernie knew he would have to use other means in getting the land he wanted at Fort Lawton. At a meeting he announced, "I am going to contact the National Congress of American Indians to see if they can find a way to help us."

When the National Congress of American Indians learned of the problems Bernie faced, they contacted the Bureau of Indian Affairs. They requested that the land at Fort Lawton be frozen at the federal level so that nobody could give it to anyone until all aspects of the transfer were studied.

Bernie told his followers, "Freezing any land transfers is the power we needed to make the mayor and the city of Seattle realize we are playing hardball. I want them to understand that they won't get any land until we get a share of it."

The mayor and the city council were left powerless and realized they had to deal with the UIATF before they could get any land.

During that time Bernard met Tom McLaughlin, the deputy regional director of the U.S. Department of Health, Education, and Welfare Region X. Tom's help became important to Bernie over the following months. They trusted each other and became close friends. Later Bernie met Buck Kelley, the regional director of the same organization. Because of Tom McLaughlin's support, Kelley accepted the UIATF application for part of the property prior to the city's application through the Department of Interior for all of the property.

The General Services Administration, responsible for the final disposition of federal surplus property, ordered the U.S. Department of Health, Education, and Welfare and the Department of Interior to order their counterparts, the UIATF and the City of Seattle, respectively, to negotiate and submit a single application before any property would be transferred.

While the efforts to negotiate with the city took place, Bernie had dozens of Indians maintaining day-and-night vigil at the main entrance gate to Fort Lawton. He wanted the city officials to understand that the UIATF was resolved to make this a long and determined fight. During the vigil several non-Indians came with food and coffee and offered their support. It soon became obvious that Bernie had caught the city officials by surprise. They had underestimated Bernie's ability and determination, as well as his knowledge of politics and the support that would grow among sympathetic non-Indians.

The city officials now realized they could not access any of the land until they worked with the UIATF. After months of negotiations, an agreement was finally reached. Twenty acres of land would be leased to the UIATF for ninety-nine years. During the meeting with the mayor's

Henry "Scoop" Jackson, U.S. senator from Washington; Joyce Reyes, president of American Indian Women's Service League; Tom McLaughlin, deputy regional director of the Department of Health, Education, and Welfare; Bernie Whitebear; and Wes Uhlman, mayor of Seattle, 1971. *Courtesy United Indians of All Tribes Foundation*

office and the city council, Bernie stated in no uncertain terms, "I do not consider this a treaty. History has proven that white people do not keep their word or honor treaties. This is a legal and binding agreement."

Bernie was aware that the locations of battlefields with the white man had changed. Fighting for Indians' rights would now take place in a different way. They would no longer be fought on the open plains or in the mountains, as before. They would be fought in the corporate headquarters or in the halls of the ways and means committees. Sometimes they would be fought in courtrooms. Attorneys dressed in three-piece suits wearing wing tip oxfords would replace warriors stripped to breechcloth with war paint on their faces. Bernie understood that times had changed and new ways would be needed to deal with the ever-changing politics and policies of the white man.

There were important victories for Indians in the 1970s. In 1971 Bernie had officially received the twenty acres of land at Fort Lawton for his proposed cultural center. In 1974 U.S. District Court Judge George Boldt ruled that the tribes were entitled to one-half of the harvestable salmon running their traditional waters. The tribes became comanagers of Washington's fisheries. This would prove to be a notable achievement for the tribes of western Washington.

Wheeling and Dealing

Bernie and his staff recognized from the beginning that funds had to be raised continually to cover the costs of operating programs. It would be difficult, and they would be constantly vying with other Indian and ethnic organizations for funding. The first order of business would be to create a slide show with audio of Indian leaders explaining the merits of an Indian cultural center.

I worked with others to lay out the initial format for the slide show. After that was put together, Chief Dan George, the movie actor, was asked to participate and voice important passages. The forty-five-minute slide show covered Indian history in Washington State and expertly explained the goals of the UIATF in creating programs to help urban Indians achieve a better quality of life.

Architectural designs and drawings and a model were created by Arai-Jackson Architects to illustrate what the cultural center would look like. I worked with them on the specifics so they could design around them. Bernie wanted to make it clear to non-Indians that the Indian cultural center would also benefit them. It could serve as a place of learning and history for everyone.

The slide show was presented to members of the Ways and Means Committee in Olympia, the state capital, and to members of Congress in Washington, D.C. Bernie and his staff presented the slide show to anyone who might be able to contribute to their cause. As time went on, this technique proved effective in raising large amounts of money.

It became obvious to Bernie that he would have to find whatever support he could. In May 1970 he learned that a convention was to be held in Chicago to allow minorities to voice their problems in the country. Bernie requested time to speak on behalf of the Indians in Seattle. At the large convention hall he heard that Carol Willis, who was to be the July playmate of the month for *Playboy*, was scheduled to speak on behalf of Indians. He learned that she was half Indian.

Bernie found the table where she was seated with others and realized Hugh Hefner was among them. He introduced himself and shared the problems he was facing in Seattle. Bernie found Hefner cordial and unassuming and willing to help out in any way he could. He suggested sending Carol, along with a chaperone, Dee Adanti, to Seattle to help raise funds. Bernie thanked Hefner for his help and called me long distance to see if I would be able to provide a room for the two while they were in Seattle. I did not believe a word coming from Bernie's mouth that day, but I agreed to provide lodging to anyone, especially if they resembled a Playboy playmate. It was not until Carol and Dee arrived at my front door in July, with packed suitcases, that I realized the truth of the matter.

Earlier Bernie had contacted the owner of the My Place Lounge near SeaTac Airport. The lounge adjoined a large dance hall. The owner and Bernie agreed to split the profits of drinks sold if the playmate would spend at least three hours mingling with the expected crowd and dancing with anyone who wished to dance with her. Radio stations in Seattle announced the event, which was designed to bring in many young men wanting to see firsthand a centerfold playmate. Bernie sent a dozen tough-looking Indians to look after Carol Willis that night. Many drinks were consumed in the lounge as men struggled to get close to the stunningly beautiful playmate.

This was the first of Bernie's fundraising exploits. Another occurred months later, when the singer Buffy St. Marie came to Seattle to perform and help with raising more money for Bernie. The night after her performance, she asked Bernie if he had a car available to pick up two friends at the SeaTac Airport. Bernie advised that he could borrow his sister Luana's two-door Chevy Nova. Bernie and Buffy drove to the airport to pick up her friends, who turned out to be Wilt Chamberlain, the pro basketball player, who was seven foot two, and another teammate,

Washington Governor Dan Evans at his desk with Peter Schnurman and Bernie Whitebear, Olympia, ca. 1975. *Courtesy United Indians of All Tribes Foundation*

who was six foot ten. The two expressed concern when they saw how small Luana's car was. Bernie got out of the driver's seat and watched Chamberlain and his teammate struggle to get into the back seat of Luana's small Nova. As the four traveled north to downtown Seattle, Bernie had difficulty seeing the traffic behind him because Chamberlain and his teammate, who were hunched over with their knees nearly touching their chins, blocked his view.

I found this experience of Bernie's amusing when I thought of how small Luana's car actually was. Other exploits continued for another thirty years.

Bernie received initial funding from Washington, and additional funds and donations came from local corporations and Indian tribes. The Quinault tribe donated the cedar shakes for the roof of the proposed cultural center. The Colville Tribe donated five truckloads of logs that formed the perimeter support of the building.

Lucy Covington, the chairman of the Colville Confederated Tribes, was at the site with Bernie when the logs arrived. Lucy was very much respected by the Colville Tribe. Everyone knew that she was the granddaughter of Chief Moses, the last recognized chief of the Colville Tribe. For some time Lucy had been a strong supporter of Bernie's, and she was pleased that the tribe could support the UIATF by supplying something that was a part of the reservation. Lucy admired Bernie for being able to get land in an urban area for the sole use of Indians. She told Bernie more than once that he should come back to the reservation and help run the affairs of the Colville Confederated Tribes.

In 1975, after five years of service to the Seattle Indian community, Peter Schnurman went to work for the UIATF on a full-time basis. Bernie and Peter worked closely and traveled together on several important business trips. They canvassed the halls of the State Capitol in Olympia and Congress in Washington, D.C., to seek funding for the UIATF. Peter was effective in raising money for the foundation's operation. The two became inseparable. In the *Spokesman Review*, a Spokane newspaper, an article appeared about the two of them. Bernie was referred to as "Bernie Schnubear."

Bernie had a favorite story about Schnurman that he enjoyed sharing. Peter had arrived in Seattle on March 8, 1970, the day Bernie and his followers raided Fort Lawton. He had come from New York City to be the director of the American Jewish Committee in Seattle. Relatives warned Peter before he left his hometown that there were still many wild Indian savages in Washington, including Seattle. Peter scoffed at their warnings as nonsense. After all, it was now 1970. Everyone knew the U.S. Cavalry had beaten the savages over a century ago.

After arriving in Seattle, Peter entered his room in the Olympic Hotel and turned on the television to view the six o'clock news. He was dumbfounded to see hundreds of Indians invading Fort Lawton and scuffling with the military police behind their leader, Bernie Whitebear. He immediately telephoned his wife, Hinda, back in New York City. "Hey, there are still wild Indians out here," he cried out. "I can't believe it."

Bernie's methods of fighting for Indian rights soon won the respect and support of U.S. Senator Henry M. Jackson. He admired Bernie's track record at the Seattle Indian Health Board. As time went on, Senator Jackson's support became invaluable, opening doors not only in Olympia but also in various offices and departments in Washington, D.C.

On May 13, 1977, the Daybreak Star Center was opened. Over three thousand people attended the grand opening. The center was paid for

Daybreak Star Center, Discovery Park, Seattle, 1977. *Courtesy Arai-Jackson Architects*

from a variety of federal and city sources, including the Seattle Office of Economic Development. May 13 was my birthday, and Bernie wanted to pay tribute to my efforts in authoring the philosophy of the UIATF. He wanted to acknowledge that I had created the name Daybreak Star Center as well as my efforts in planning the facility along with Clifford Jackson and Gerald Arai, the two architects who designed the beautiful center.

Bernie received many words of praise that day. Mom was especially proud of him. She gave a short talk to the grateful audience and thanked them for assisting her son for the last seven years. All the Indians in Seattle were pleased they finally had a place to call their own. To many it became known as "the house that Bernie built."

The Daybreak Star Center, a twenty-thousand-square-foot building, was a beautiful structure. The Seattle *Post-Intelligencer* described it as a work of art. The building's design was inspired by the words of Black Elk, the great Lakota holy man:

> Then as I stood there two men were coming from the East head first like arrows flying and between them rose the Daybreak Star. They

came and gave an herb to me and said "with this on earth you shall undertake anything and do it." It was the daybreak star herb, the herb of understanding and they told me to drop it on the earth. I saw it falling far and when it struck the earth it rooted and grew and flowered four blossoms on one stem, a black, a white, a scarlet, and a yellow. And the rays from these streamed upward to the heavens so that all creatures saw it and in no place was there darkness.

The building was contemporary in design but it had a character that drew from traditional Indian motifs from across the country. The interior walls were adorned by enormous artworks created by the leading Indian artists of the nation. The funds of eighty thousand dollars to pay for the artwork came from Bernie's efforts as a member of the Seattle Arts Commission. Earlier, members of the commission led by Morrie Alhadeff, Bernie's friend and the owner of the Longacres Racetrack, suggested to Mayor Uhlman that he appoint Bernie as a new commissioner.

After the Daybreak Star Center opened, Bernie finally had a place close to his heart and close to nature to throw his pow wows. The Great Circle, situated near the Daybreak Star Center, was a large circle covered with grass. The surrounding hillside was terraced so the spectators could sit at different levels to enjoy the event. The pow wow was held each year during the last weekend in July, beginning on Friday night and ending Sunday evening. The crowds were enormous, and some of the greatest singers, dancers, and drummers of the Plains and Plateau Indians performed. As the pow wows took place, everyone enjoyed watching the bald eagles as they exercised their aerial acrobatics in the sky above. They graced the sky with their presence during every pow wow.

Hundreds of dancers, singers, and drummers from all parts of North America came to participate. Thousands of spectators from as far as Europe and Asia and all over the United States enjoyed the pow wows as much as the Indians. Sometimes, they joined in the dances that were not difficult to perform, such as the Round Dance.

During the pow wows Bernie and his close friend, Victor Johns, a Tlingit from Whitehorse Yukon Territory, served Indian-style salmon

Victor Johns in
Discovery Park,
Seattle, 1977.
*Courtesy United
Indians of All Tribes
Foundation*

baked over alder. Each day hundreds of people formed lines to sample
it. Over the years it became commonplace to see Victor and Bernie
working side by side. Sometimes it was hard to locate Bernie because
he was short. But if one could spot Victor, who was a head taller than
Bernie, it was certain that "Bear" would be nearby. This was Vic's often-
used nickname that he had coined for his good friend. When the pow
wows were in session the two handled all matters that had to be attended to: security, transportation of elders, and the pickup and deliv-
ery of all supplies.

Since the Daybreak Star Center was completed thousands of visitors
have come. Many came to appreciate the beautiful design of the building. Others came to view the unique artwork and artifacts of tribes
throughout the country that had been gifted to the UIATF.

On some evenings Bernie threw special dinners at the Daybreak Star

Center. Young Indians presented and modeled beautifully made traditional Indian costumes and attire. Soft drumming provided the background to these shows. At other times the Cape Fox Dancers performed under the direction of Cecelia White. They were dressed in the beautiful attire of the Tlingit, and they sang and drummed selected works of their tribe and their region. The audiences always loved their performances. On other evenings, the Sacred Circle Gallery presented the artwork of Indian artists at special shows. Over the years many Indian artists benefited from the sales and promotions of the gallery.

The Daybreak Star Center has served as a popular place for various functions: intertribal meetings, dinner theaters, salmon feasts, and more than one hundred fifty marriage ceremonies. Most functions were sold out. Those running for political office sponsored numerous shrimp feeds and clambakes. During certain parts of the year non-Indians used the Daybreak Star Center as much as Indians, hosting everything from banquets and conventions to dance classes and musical presentations.

The many tribes that lived in Seattle now had a common place to get to know each other and share their unique cultures. Daybreak Star Center became a home away from home for many. Those tribes that were once traditional enemies buried their animosities of the past and shared in the common good. The many tribes had come together and literally formed a new tribe, the UIATF, where customs, languages, singing and dancing styles, and traditional foods were shared.

Later the Yale Building on Eastlake Avenue in Seattle was acquired, paid for by a million-dollar grant acquired from the state. This was the result of one of Bernie's greatest fundraising coups, which occurred in 1975 at the State Capitol. Ten years later the Yale Building and property it sat on had quadrupled in value.

Bernie was successful in acquiring other valuable buildings and land that became the property of the UIATF. The Broderick Building, along with adjoining property, was one of them. It was located on Second Avenue and Cherry Street in downtown Seattle. It housed the administrative offices of the UIATF for several years. The city had originally bought the building and property. Later it was given to the Seattle Indian Services Commission that was made up of four Indian organizations: American Indian Women's Service League, Seattle Indian

Health Board, The Indian Center, and UIATF. The commission agreed that the UIATF would manage the building and the property. Bernie assigned Peter Schnurman that responsibility.

Later, the La-ba-te-yah Youth Home was funded after Bernie took title to a large building on an acre of land in the Crown Hill area, north of Seattle. Funding came from a Federal Housing and Urban Development grant for 2.1 million dollars. The grant was the biggest given in the nation that year. The city came up with additional money to operate the building, and the state added funds to help renovate it. All told, the amount of money received for the building, land, and renovation added up to 2.8 million dollars. I was always amazed at how Bernie was able to get state agencies to come up with funds.

The building housed the La-ba-te-yah Youth Program that cared for hundreds of troubled teenagers from the reservations. During these years thousands of young Indians were aided. They received help in getting a higher education, on-the-job training, and jobs. Many who had problems with alcohol received help and counseling at the Thunder-Bird House, a facility with trained staff who could deal with alcoholism.

Another important facility housed the I' Wa' Sil Youth Program that serviced other young Indians whose problems were less severe. The Substance Abuse Center administered outpatient treatment for Indians who were having problems with alcohol and drugs. It educated Indians in the prevention of these illnesses. There was an Elder's Service that provided meals and a place where older people could socialize and enjoy programs designed for their age group.

On several occasions, Bernie rode in Seattle police cars at night. He wanted to make sure the police were sensitive to Indians with drinking problems. At one hearing with the Seattle Police Department, Bernie stated, "Remember, it isn't that Indians can't handle alcohol, they simply can't handle this life."

Once Bernie had a steady income, he rented a large house with six bedrooms near Green Lake. He shared space in his home with many Indians who could not afford their own accommodations. Many were young adults who were attending the University of Washington, Seattle University, or one of the community colleges in the area. Others were from various reservations around the country and simply down and out. Sometimes these people were housed free of charge at Bernie's home for days or weeks.

Our family attended many salmon bakes at Bernie's house. If Bernie was not baking the salmon, Vic Johns would be doing the honors. There were always many people visiting him. It was a great place to assemble because of its size and closeness to Green Lake.

Bernie contributed generously from his own pocket to pay for food and other expenses that seemed to always be needed by his guests. When his personal finances were depleted, he borrowed from his family to help pay the expenses of others. Over the years this became a habit — to the dismay of Bernie's brothers and sisters. Bernie had never been able to save any money for himself because he was always loaning it or giving it to Indians whom he felt needed it more.

During these years Bernie's constant companion was Marilyn Sieber. She was a member of the Nit Nat Tribe located near Victoria, British Columbia. Marilyn worked tirelessly helping Bernie in running the UIATF and setting up programs. They worked hard and played hard together for more than ten years.

Several times Bernie and Marilyn visited penitentiaries in Washington, namely Monroe, Walla Walla, and Purdy. His goal was to counsel young Indian inmates. He wanted them to know that they were not forgotten and something positive was waiting for them on the outside once their sentences were served. He kept his promise for many of them and found employment for those who wanted jobs. Some found jobs at the UIATF. Because of his efforts Bernie gained respect and made many friends among the young inmates.

One weekend as they were driving past Snoqualmie Pass, Bernie and Marilyn stopped to watch the skiers coming down the mountain.

"I'll bet Indian kids would enjoy this sport," Bernie predicted.

"If they could afford it and someone could teach them, it would be great," Marilyn agreed.

The next weekend Bernie was on a pair of skis. He wanted to get good enough so he could teach others. After reaching the top of a small incline via a rope tow, Marilyn watched Bernie closely as he faced his first challenge on skis. He was hunched over his ski poles close to the snow with his head down. His legs were spread far apart as he snowplowed the incline at a snail's pace. It was amusing for our family to watch Bernie learn to ski. We could see the determination in his dark penetrating eyes.

"I think you should work on your style and technique, Bernie, before you start teaching anyone," Marilyn suggested. "I would hate to see Indian kids skiing like you."

Bernie continued practicing until he felt he was ready. He was able to locate funds to take two-dozen Indian kids skiing one weekend. Money needed to pay for their lunches came from Bernie's own pocket. Every winter for several years, whenever money could be raised, Bernie and Marilyn took young Indian kids from Seattle and taught them the rudiments of skiing at Snoqualmie Pass. The youngsters would never forget this experience. Bernie felt it important to let young Indians experience activities on a playfield that had been traditionally reserved for whites. He felt this would help enlarge the scope of life for Indian kids and help them reach out further.

One day several friends were seated in their favorite restaurant and watering hole, Louie's, in the Ballard area when someone remarked, "It's too bad that Bernie never had kids of his own." Another stated adamantly, "What do you mean? He has a bigger family than anyone I know. He actually has thousands of kids. Every Indian kid in Seattle is, in one way or another, Bernie's. I don't know of any adult who has received more love and respect from the young ones than the Bear."

It was true that Bernie enjoyed being around young people. He felt good about being able to contribute something good to their growth. It was a privilege to give them something that he never had when he was young. More than once he had considered getting married and having a family of his own. He announced one time, at a large gathering, that Marilyn Sieber and he were planning to get married in the fall of that year. Many of his friends thought that it would be good for him, but it did not happen.

As the months, then years, passed Bernie became completely involved with the leadership of the UIATF. Leading the organization took almost all of his time. He realized that there would never be enough time to have a family and direct the UIATF at the same time.

When Luana and I had children, Bernie was pleased with the new additions to the family. He gave much attention to my son and daughter, Darren and Lara, and Luana's daughter, Kecia. For their birthdays he always made sure there were presents. When Christmas came, meaningful gifts were always under the tree for them.

During the years when our children were going through adolescence, they learned that they could always get money from their Uncle Bernie when they needed it. This same pattern of exchanging money occurred when Darren's daughter, Gaby, was born and Lara's daughter, Recy, followed two years later. Gaby and Recy seemed to know instinctively where to get money. Because their great-uncle was usually broke, he, in turn, learned where to get the money his great-nieces wanted. He would come to Luana and me and ask for a loan. After getting the money, he went to the children and graciously gave them the amount they needed. Over the years Luana and I were never the wiser.

On Memorial Day, 1978, our family was stunned when our mother was killed in an automobile accident near the Washington–Idaho border on I-90. The wake was held at the Catholic Church in Inchelium the night before the burial at Pia, bordering the Kettle River. Hundreds of tribal members attended. At least three-dozen of my mother's friends and admirers came from Seattle and Tacoma. A number of elders from the Inchelium area who came to the funeral were still fluent in the Sin-Aikst language. Many knew and respected Mom's father, Pic Ah Kelowna, White Grizzly Bear. They were pleased to meet Bernie. Many of them had heard about him, and they were proud of his efforts to help Indians. I watched all of them with interest as they told Bernie that he had a strong resemblance to Mom's father.

Mom's death was a huge loss for the family. We loved her very much. We were fully aware that we all came from her. Our love for Mom was matched only by our admiration for her strength, her determination, and her love. After returning to Seattle, Bernie buried himself in his work. The sadness of Mom's passing would always be with him, but he knew the importance of his mission.

Bernie knew the value of networking. During the mid-1970s he joined forces with Bob Santos, executive director of Inter*Im representing the Asian community, Roberto Maestas, executive director of El Centro de la Raza representing the Latino community, and Larry

Our mother, Mary Christian, Tacoma, 1954.

The Gang of Four, Roberto Maestas, Bernie Whitebear, Larry Gossett, and Bob Santos, at Union Station, Seattle, 1997. *Courtesy Audrey Pray*

Gossett, executive director of the Central Area Motivation Program representing the black community. The organization of these four men was officially known as The Minority Executive Directors Coalition of King County. They became dear to the communities they represented and were affectionately called the "Gang of Four."

The Gang of Four worked closely together for many years, supporting each other in their goals to better the quality of life for their communities. The four attended meetings of the Seattle city council to present funding requests for their own agencies and to support proposals submitted by the others. Their unity proved to be an effective show of force.

During the fall each year, the Gang of Four took part in the Community Show-Off, sponsored by the Northwest Asian American Theatre in Seattle. Performances were given by many people representing the various ethnic groups. There was singing, dancing, skits, and music played on an assortment of instruments. The event was usually presented at the Nippon Kan Theater near the International District. The performances were always interesting and enlightening.

The Gang of Four always participated at the Community Show-Offs, and they usually stole the show as they performed their song-and-dance routines. One of their most popular performances was when they mimicked Gladys Knight and the Pips, with a friend, Annie Galarosa, singing the lead.

Bernie learned years before, when he played Sitting Bull in "Annie Get Your Gun," that he had the ability to capture the attention of audiences. The Community Show-Offs gave him the opportunity to perform and make people laugh. He loved to do this. He also made many friends and admirers in several ethnic communities made up of Chinese, Japanese, Filipinos, Mexicans, and blacks. As time passed, Bernie learned he could count on these people to support him.

When Bernie was able to afford it, he hired people who were expert grant writers. He was not shy about canvassing the State Capitol in Olympia to search for funding. Soon he learned where to go in Washington, D.C., to do the same thing. He and members of his growing staff did this continuously.

On one of his first trips to Washington, D.C., he met U.S. Senator Daniel Inouye and made a strong ally. Later they became friends. Over the years Senator Inouye was very effective in giving support to American Indians all over the United States. Inouye was considered a hero to many Indians across the country. When Governor Dan Evans became the U.S. Senator for Washington, Bernie kept in close contact with him. Over the years a strong feeling of trust and respect was formed between them. This was also true of Patty Murray when she later became the U.S. Senator for Washington.

Bernie hired Bob Kendrick and Bob Keller to write grants for the UIATF. John McNab joined them later, offering strong administrative and grant-writing abilities. These men were responsible for bringing in larger grants. In 1984 Bernie hired Jamie Garner, an attorney, to help him with legal matters. For fourteen years Jamie was one of the ablest grant writers for the UIATF. These gifted men wrote up the request for grants, and Bernie made the oral presentations. Working in concert, they brought in a lot of money to the UIATF.

As programs were created, Bernie and his staff went in search of money to fund them. Eventually, the funds brought in exceeded 124 million dollars. The Ina Maka Family Program sponsored the foster care of Indian children and it provided cultural and clinical care, when needed. Another program sponsored education and employment services for Indians who had recently come to Seattle from Indian reservations needing help in adjusting to urban living. A Child Development Center was established to help young Indian children when they entered public schools in the Seattle area. Head Start and Early Childhood Education and Assistance Programs were established and became popular, serving dozens of youngsters annually. A GED Testing Center aided those who were getting the equivalent to a high school diploma. The Sacred Circle Art Gallery had exhibitions of Indian artists on a regular basis and received critical attention throughout the year. There was a monthly art market where arts and crafts were displayed and sold to the public.

From the beginning Bernie was ably assisted by Joyce Reyes, director of Title IV, Joan LaFrance, director of curriculum development, and Bobbie Conner, director of communications. The three helped organize and direct the operations of the many programs that were being formed. At times one or the other would attend meetings in Washington, D.C., to benefit the needs of the UIATF when Bernie was unable to do it.

By the mid-1980s the Daybreak Star Center was a very busy place. The staff numbered over one hundred twenty. Each day eight busses and vans transported young and old to the center to attend classes and programs designed for them. The activities at the Daybreak Star Center drew many.

Often Bernie and his staff could be found working late at night, preparing for the next day's classes and programs. More than once he allowed the guards who were scheduled to watch over the center go home to celebrate personal events. Several times he relieved the guards and spent time by himself guarding the Daybreak Star Center on New

Year's Eve. When friends of his, including Bob Santos, learned of this, they would drive out with a bottle of bourbon and spend the night with him, toasting each other and the year to come.

After Bernie won the land for the UIATF in 1971, Bob Satiacum parted company with him and proceeded to face other challenges and win victories of his own. He became involved in selling tax-free cigarettes, and he continued to be involved in fishing for salmon, although he paid others to do it for him. Bob also set up a large cocktail lounge near Portland Avenue. It became so popular that there was usually standing room only. Indians, non-Indians, friends, and foes all gathered to give Bob business. Within a few years he became very wealthy.

Occasionally I would drive down to Tacoma and visit him. He no longer lived in his old fishing shack but in a luxurious home on a quarter acre. The backyard had a large swimming pool with a retractable roof for year-round use. The smell of fish that was so much a part of his old house was noticeably missing. When I drove into Bob's front yard I saw the many cars he owned, a beautiful black Lincoln Continental that seemed half a block long, an elegant Rolls Royce, and two Firebirds.

During the evening the two of us went downtown and drank at several cocktail lounges Bob frequented. Everyone seemed to know him. I realized that many white people who did not like him before liked him even less now that he had made it. They seemed to resent his newly acquired wealth. When Bob saw them, he smiled and offered to buy them a drink. No one took the offer.

The state also resented Bob's success. He had always been a thorn in their side, and they tried very hard to find a way to beat him. Eventually, they indicted him on the nonpayment of taxes. Bob realized he could not win in court, and he went into hiding in Canada and remained there for five years. He was finally caught in a remote village in British Columbia when the Canadian mounted police traced a telephone call he made to relatives in Tacoma. When the police realized he was hiding out only two blocks from their headquarters, they surrounded the house and barged through the door. Bob was seated, having a beer and watching television. He looked up, smiled, and offered them a seat. He calmly asked, "What kept you guys?"

Bob was imprisoned in Vancouver, British Columbia, and Bernie and

I traveled there several times to visit him. During the spring of 1985, Bob Satiacum called upon Bernie to speak on his behalf to the court in Vancouver. Bob wanted the judge there to know that he had the backing of many Indians in Washington. Bernie spoke to the court, and several Indians from British Columbia who supported Bob were at the hearings.

Unfortunately, Bernie's efforts were in vain, but he impressed the Indians there. They had never heard an Indian who could express himself so well. From the beginning, the Canadian Indians fared poorly with the white people. The oppression against Indians was more severe in Canada than it was in the United States. After meeting Bernie, their leaders improved in expressing themselves and stating their cases. Within years Indian leaders throughout Canada spoke up for their needs and started to make important gains for their people.

In March 1991 Bob Satiacum died at the prison in Vancouver. Bernie was not surprised when he learned this. He knew that the Great Spirit did not mean Indians to be imprisoned. They were a people that needed to be free. Bob was finally able to return to his homeland in Tacoma, in a casket, free of the harassment from the state. A memorial was held in his honor as hundreds came to pay their last respect. Both friends and enemies came.

White people, for the most part, did not like Bob but they did respect him. They knew that he was a force to contend with. Many whites had difficulty accepting that an Indian would stand up for his rights as a human being so forcefully for such a long time. Bernie knew Bob's life and death were not in vain. Bob had fought for Indian's rights most of his life and he suffered much abuse from white people during that time. Bob Satiacum contributed greatly to winning the battles of Indian fishing rights in Washington. In the beginning, he did this almost single-handedly.

The Boldt Decision in 1974 was handed down for the most part because of Bob's unconditional stance on the issue. The victories benefited thousands of Indians who made up the western Washington tribes. Bernie was proud of his friendship with Bob. He was honored to have fished and fought alongside him during the late 1950s and most of the 1960s. Bernie considered Bob Satiacum as a courageous individual who was always seeking justice for his people. He looked upon Bob as an unrelenting modern-day warrior. Bernie had received an important education from Bob regarding the plight of the western Washington tribes. He hoped that young Indians of the future would remember Bob's courage and look upon him as a special role model.

> "We have a rich culture in Seattle
>
> and Bernie was one of the crown jewels."
>
> —Ron Sims, King County executive

The Tribute

At five o'clock on November 1, 1997, it was nearly dark. There was a hint of moisture in the air, and the soft winds passing through felt warm and inviting. It had not rained for days, and it felt good to be outside. People were everywhere, walking and milling about on Jackson Street. It was always like this when the weather was good. Most of the people in the area were Asian, but many whites and blacks could be seen here and there waiting at bus stops or passing through to other parts of the city.

Several staff members of the UIATF were already at Union Station near Fourth and Jackson. A few UIATF board members were there, also. They showed concern that word had not been released early enough for the night's event. They were worried that the Union Station banquet hall was too large and only a part of it would be filled for Bernie Whitebear's tribute.

On September 2, 1997, Bernie had been admitted to Swedish Hospital in Ballard for surgery. The surgeons had discovered a severe case of colon cancer. Friends of Bernie had noticed his dramatic loss of weight. He usually weighed a hundred eighty-five pounds, but within weeks he was down to a hundred thirty. The doctor's diagnosis was not good— Bernie had only months to live, five months at most. The Seattle *Times* did a front-page story on Bernie's life and triumphs over the years and discussed his present condition. Many in Seattle were surprised. Many in the Indian communities of Seattle, Tacoma, and outlying areas were dismayed by the news.

Bernie Whitebear,
Seattle, 1997.
Courtesy Ben Marra

The staff of the UIATF had planned the evening's event. They wanted to honor Bernie, to pay tribute to him, while he was still well, for all of his efforts and accomplishments over the past thirty years. Everyone in the Indian community knew that Bernie had tirelessly devoted his life to improving the quality of life for Indians in Seattle. This would be a celebration to honor him for what he had done, not only for Indians, but for other minority groups who had faced neglect from the city and the state in the past.

At five-thirty the crowds of people entering Union Station began to grow noticeably. The round tables were beginning to be filled as more people entered the large banquet hall. The number of people who came to pay tribute to my brother impressed me. Shortly after six o'clock every table had been taken and people continued to enter the hall. Nearly two hundred were left without a place to sit and had to stand in the foyer and in the back of the large hall. No one wanted to leave.

There was a cross-section of people in the hall that included Asians, whites, blacks, Latinos, and Indians. Several represented city, county, and state governments, including Governor Gary Locke and former Governor Mike Lowry. The hall that had seemed too large at first now appeared too small as more people entered searching for a place to sit.

When Bernie appeared, friends surrounded him. Those who supported him over the years came up to pay their respects. The attitude of the large crowd changed when Bernie entered the hall. Before he appeared the hall was morose, but now everyone was in a festive mood. Bernie had always had the ability to make people feel better, and it proved to be true that night. I was pleased at Bernie's ability to do this, and I was always surprised at his innate power to accomplish goals and overcome barriers that were set before him.

Hattie Kaufmann had taken time off from her job on "Good Morning America" in New York City to emcee the event for the evening. Hattie was half Nez Perce, and many in the crowd knew her and appreciated her professionalism. She told the crowd, "We are here tonight to honor a very special person who has helped many over the years. There are those who will talk tonight on his behalf and relate warm personal stories about this man. I hope you will enjoy yourselves at this very special event tonight honoring Bernie Whitebear."

Over a dozen speakers paid tribute to Bernie that night. Near the end Governor Locke and former Governor Lowry took the stage. After reading a proclamation honoring Bernie, Governor Locke declared the month of November 1997 as Bernie Whitebear Month. The crowd applauded. Then Governor Locke declared Bernie the First Citizen of the Decade in Washington. The crowd rose as one to give Bernie a standing ovation.

The ovation did not end until Bernie took the stage. He looked at the crowd and spotted Bob Santos, his old friend and one of the Gang of Four. Bernie said, "Bob, I'm going to enlist you, Maestas, and Gossett as my pallbearers. Over the years I've had to carry you guys. Now it's close to the time when you'll have to carry me." The crowd knew of their closeness and enjoyed the humor between them.

Bernie studied the crowd for a minute and said, "While we are here tonight, I feel I should share the prognosis of my doctor." Bernie paused. He looked very frail and drawn. Everyone listened attentively, showing concern and deep respect. The crowd was on the edge of their seats. Bernie went on, "After my surgery one of my doctors told me that I had serious colon cancer. Half of my liver was consumed with the cancer, and it had reached my blood supply, the doctor said." Grim faced, Bernie replied, "With all due respect, Doctor, I would like a second opinion." The doctor studied Bernie for a minute and sighed, "Well, alright, you're ugly, too."

I could see that the joke caught the crowd off-guard. There was complete quiet in the large banquet hall for a moment, then everyone realized Bernie was playing with them as he always had in the past. There was a roar of laughter, and everyone in the hall relaxed. The tension was gone, and everyone knew that everything would be fine. I smiled as I watched Bernie make people feel better. He had always had this ability and his humor had always served him well over the years.

The tribute lasted five hours. Afterward Bernie, accompanied by family, friends, and Mike Lowry, went to the lounge of the Bush Garden in the International District. While everyone indulged in a favorite drink, Bernie had a pot of tea.

"He was an edge walker who could cross
cultures, explain and inspire without sacrificing
his own identity."

—Paul Schell, mayor of Seattle

Loose Ends

During the following months Bernie worked his usual sched-
ule. Much of his energy was devoted to the design and planning of the
People's Lodge. This great structure would be his last gift to the Indian
people.

Drawings prepared and submitted by Clifford Jackson and Jerry Arai,
the architects and designers of the Daybreak Star Center, were studied
and reviewed. They were pinned to the wall in Bernie's bedroom so he
could study them from his bed throughout the day. If something did
not appear right, Bernie made notes of things that had to be changed.

New difficulties arose later when the designs and requirements met
resistance from the Magnolia Community Club in Seattle. They felt the
design of the building was too large and would require excessive parking. They did not want an Indian structure that large on land that they
still considered their personal park. Other difficulties arose when Bernie
learned that the city reneged on the 1972 agreement. It was changed in
1982, stating that a museum could not be built in Discovery Park. Years
of effort in planning, designing, and consultation would be wasted if
the city would not agree with what the UIATF wanted and needed in
the structures of the People's Lodge.

Bernie was sometimes distracted from his efforts in Seattle. He was
on the board of directors of the National Museum of the American
Indian in Washington, D.C. Architects, planners, and the board were
deeply involved in the planning of this monumental museum, which
was scheduled to open in 2004. Because of the scope of the project,

Bernie had to make several trips to Washington, D.C., to attend important meetings. The site of the new museum would be the last six acres in the Smithsonian complex. The beautiful structure designed by Douglas Cardinal, a Blackfoot architect from Canada, would be constructed directly across the mall from the East Wing Museum of Modern Art. Both museums would be adjacent to the nation's Capitol Building. Close to a million artifacts from the Heye Collection in New York City were being catalogued and stored in preparation for the museum's grand opening.

I knew this was a project close to Bernie's heart. He had met and made friends with other members of the board, and he collaborated well with the director, Rick West, and his staff. Bernie got to work closely with his old friend, Vine Deloria Jr., who was also on the board of directors.

Bernie had visions that works from the National Collection would be shared for viewing in Seattle once the People's Lodge was completed. He felt this would be very important for Seattle in years to come. Bernie worked to make this a reality as his cancer gradually weakened him.

As busy as Bernie was with his large projects, his concern was always for others. He often drove about Seattle at night seeking Indians in need. On one of his drives late one cold and rainy night, Bernie drove past a young Indian who was sleeping on a bench at a bus stop. Bernie stopped his van. As he swung open the passenger door, he called out to the young man, "Need a place to stay for the night?" Gratefully, the boy hopped into the heated van. The next day Bernie brought the teenager to the La-Ba-Te-Yah Youth Home near Crown Hill. The young boy, Mike Quill, was in awe that a leader such as Bernie Whitebear would take the time to do this for him.

I attended a special awards dinner months later. Mike spoke in front of a large audience at the Daybreak Star Center. It was obvious that he was nervous speaking in front of so many adults and strangers. He told of Bernie's deed. He said Bernie's effort enabled him to see the good in people and to trust in their intentions. Bernie, he said, not only offered help but instilled a feeling of hope.

Before Bernie began treatment for his illness, he went down to Auburn, Washington, to speak on behalf of the Muckleshoot Tribe. Over the years he had made friends in the tribe. At the time the Muckle-shoots were in the process of developing a large amphitheater in the Auburn area, but there was much dissension from the white community living there. At a public hearing Bernie gave emotional testimony in support of the project, in the process making more friends in the Muckleshoot Tribe.

Bernie's initial treatment was administered at the University of Washington Hospital. Chemotherapy was taken weekly. For four months the treatment lowered Bernie's cancer count, but then the cancer count rose. Bernie was treated with another chemotherapy. Again the cancer count was lowered, but within three months it rose again. A third chemotherapy was administered with the same results. I had accompanied Bernie on some of his visits there. After a year at the University of Washington Hospital, Bernie was advised that they could do nothing more to help him.

Later Bernie went to the Swedish Hospital on First Hill for treatment. Again the new therapy prescribed worked for a few months but then the cancer count raised and Bernie suffered. He began to lose more weight. His body grew very weak, but his mind was as sharp as ever. During his time in the hospital many came to visit and pay their respects to Bernie. One day a good-looking, well-dressed man came. He introduced himself as Dino Rossi, and he told me that Bernie had helped him when he was attending Seattle University. He told me he was grateful to Bernie because he provided him part-time employment to help him make his way. As we talked I learned that his mother was part Tlingit from Alaska. In 2004 Dino Rossi ran on the Republican ticket for governor of the State of Washington.

One day after greeting many visitors, Bernie told Luana that he needed rest and did not want to see any more people. The nurse in charge of admittance was advised to hold back all others. Not long after that, Roberto Maestas came to pay Bernie a visit. As one of the Gang of Four, Roberto was a close friend of Bernie and active in fighting for the rights of the Latino coalitions in Seattle. Roberto was stopped at admittance.

The nurse came to Bernie's room. "There's a Mr. Maestas here to see Mr. Whitebear. What do you want me to do?"

"Call the Immigration Department," Bernie shouted with an uncompromising grimace.

Many people in the Seattle area knew of the friendly rivalry between Roberto and Bernie. They had known and worked together for years fighting racial injustice. Many could relate to the humorous episodes that grew from their relationship.

Years before Bernie and some friends met at a favorite watering hole in the International District. The subject of Maestas arose that night.

"How in the hell can you tell when Maestas is lying?" someone asked.

"That's easy," Bernie responded, "when his lips are moving."

Another time when Bernie called Maestas a Mexican, Roberto responded, "If you please, Bernie. I have come up in the world. From now on refer to me as a Latino."

During the second week of February 2000, Bernie grew too weak to work at his beloved Daybreak Star Center. He had to guide the UIATF from his bedroom over the telephone. Throughout the days staff and friends came to get advice or simply visit.

The telephone rang continually. Top officials of city, county, and federal governments called to wish their best to Bernie. The press called daily to check on his condition. Senator Patty Murray, Bernie's cherished friend, called to wish Bernie well, as did Governor Gary Locke. King County Executive Ron Sims came to Bernie's house to visit. Mayor Paul Schell called to give his regards more than once. Sharon Tomeko Santos, the state representative of the 37th District, came with her husband, Bob Santos, on Sundays to prepare delicious Filipino meals for Bernie's family and friends.

On April 9, 2000, Bernie insisted on attending the UIATF board meeting at the Daybreak Star Center. He wanted to visit his old friend, Star, a purebred German Shepherd that had been given to him by his dear friend from Okanogan, Paul Schulz.

It was a touching moment when I saw Bernie enter the Daybreak Star Center in his wheelchair. Star, standing on his rear legs, could not contain himself when he saw Bernie. He placed his huge front paws on Bernie's fragile chest. He followed Bernie wherever he went.

The board of directors greeted Bernie and seated him at the confer-

Bernie Whitebear and Star at Daybreak Star Center, 1993. *Courtesy United Indians of All Tribes Foundation*

ence table with Star at his feet, and the board proceeded with the business at hand. Bernie requested permission to say a few words.

"I think it's time for me to step aside. As you can see I'm not getting around as well as I used to. I want you to know that much has been accomplished by all of us. It's been a great adventure for me." Bernie paused for a moment. His breathing was labored. Star looked up at him, and Bernie patted him gently on his head. "I hope you have enjoyed our time together as much as I have. I want you to know that I have valued your assistance a great deal over the years. You are all my friends, and that is important to me. If I can be of further help to you, call me at home. That's where I'll be for the rest of my time." He told the board that he was confident they could manage the affairs of the UIATF and that they would pursue his dreams of the People's Lodge.

Joe DeLaCruz, the longtime leader of the Quinaults and a board member, talked quietly with Bernie, discussing important issues. They had done this many times over the years, and they trusted each other's knowledge of Indian affairs. They were always close, the best of friends. Their knowledge of Indian issues was unmatched, and everyone trusted their combined wisdom. Joe assured Bernie that he would make certain that the board tended to the important matters of the UIATF.

When Bernie was assisted to the van to leave for his home, everyone knew this would be the last time he would conduct meetings in his headquarters, the Daybreak Star Center, "the house that Bernie built." The feelings of the entire board and staff were reflected in the eyes of Star as he followed Bernie's van as it departed for the last time.

As Bernie spent his last days at his home, many letters came in from around the country. Vine Deloria Jr., the respected author and educator, wrote Bernard and called him the most important Indian of the last century. Janet McCloud, a Tulalip Indian, stated in a handwritten letter that she regarded Bernie as the most effective leader ever in the Northwest. Wendy Tokuda, of Channel 5 TV in San Francisco and a former resident of Seattle, wrote a touching letter to Bernie, saying she regarded Bernie as a leader equal to any chief. Rick West, the director of the National Museum of the American Indian in Washington, D.C., sent a kind letter with a beautifully carved white bear made of ivory. Later he sent a beautiful Pendleton blanket. Within days over

Bernie Whitebear, Bob Kendrick, and Joe DeLaCruz, 1977. *Courtesy United Indians of All Tribes Foundation*

a dozen Pendleton blankets of many colors and designs arrived from friends all over the state. Dozens of letters and cards came from friends and admirers of many tribes from throughout the nation. From his bedroom Bernie continued to give directions over the telephone to his staff. Sometimes they came to his house and sat at his bedside. He struggled to battle his illness, but his doctors at the Swedish Hospital took him off chemotherapy. They wanted Bernie's last days to be as comfortable as possible.

Luana and her daughter, Kecia, flew in from Rockville, Maryland. They wanted to be there to help us care for Bernie during his last days. Teresa and Laura, our younger sisters, took turns cooking, answering the telephone, and carrying out Bernie's requests. Harry, our younger brother, worked outside maintaining Bernie's yard and running errands. I moved into Bernie's home to care for him at night.

We talked about the success and gains made by the UIATF over the years. We also talked about death. Bernie was curious of the encounters he might experience when he crossed over. He did not express a fear of dying, he was simply curious. Eleanor Kelly, a hospice worker, came to help and share professional and caring advice. She and others from hospice were always there when the family needed them. Bernie appreciated their care and involvement.

On the morning of April 16, we received shocking news. Joe DeLaCruz, Bernie's beloved friend, had died suddenly of a heart attack at the SeaTac Airport. Joe was en route to a meeting in Oklahoma. Bernie could not believe Joe was gone. He was to be one of Bernie's pallbearers. They had actually joked about it for months. We were greatly saddened by his death.

Joe DeLaCruz's memorial was held at the convention center at Ocean Shores on April 22. More than two thousand people attended. Governor Gary Locke was invited to give the opening address. He had called Bernie and invited him to fly with him to the memorial. He knew that Dorothy had asked Bernie to address the farewell to Joe. Bernie declined Governor Locke's invitation, as he felt he would be more comfortable with our family in the van.

Bernie was very thin and the pains of his cancer were severe. He never complained, and his sense of humor was still a part of him. Bernie did not reveal the pain and discomfort he was going through. All his life he had been able to mask pain, discomfort, and disappointments.

The van pulled up to the convention center. I wheeled Bernie to the front of the large hall. As we waited, drums signaled the entry of Joe's casket into the hall. Other drums echoed the beats of the drums leading to the unadorned casket of ponderosa pine. Everyone stood in quiet tribute. It was a solemn but beautiful experience for everyone. Friends, public officials, and tribal leaders reminisced about their special times with Joe.

Bernie was introduced as the final speaker, and I wheeled him to the podium. There was absolute silence in the audience. Bernie managed to climb the stairs with my help. He stood unsteadily, supported by friends behind him, as he gave his farewell address. He ended it by saying, "Like all of you I regarded Joe as my special friend. He will never be replaced. I will miss him."

When he finished everyone rose and gave Bernie a standing ovation. Dorothy, Joe's wife, walked tearfully to Bernie and embraced him as he was helped into the wheelchair. It was a touching salute from a cousin and good friend that was felt throughout the hall. It brought tears to my eyes as I watched the proceedings. Everyone knew that an important era had ended. Joe's enormous knowledge of Indian issues had been appreciated by people across the nation.

Bernie remembered the many meetings between he and Joe before the raids on Fort Lawton. They spent long hours together discussing strategy. The two agreed that the efforts at Fort Lawton could not afford to make the same mistakes that were made with the invasion of Alcatraz, which had occurred a year earlier. Both knew how important the occupation of Alcatraz was, that it had given a feeling of power and importance to all Indian people. The invasion of Alcatraz was directly tied to the attitudes of Red Power that many young Indians throughout the nation were feeling. The occupation was necessary for Indian people to try to get something back from those who had taken everything important from them. Joe and Bernie were proud of the efforts of many young Indians who were members of the American Indian Movement. They were appreciative of the foresight and determination these young men exhibited when they occupied the island.

Joe explained at length, "We have to do something different this time. Alcohol and drugs cannot be allowed. That is what hurt the people at Alcatraz. Infighting among their leaders destroyed their sense of purpose and direction. They could not keep their minds on what they were supposed to do. At the end they had no leadership that was worth a damn."

Bernie and Joe understood that the people of San Francisco, for the most part, were sympathetic to the Indians and their goals. A great deal of money and help was available to the Indians at that time. The problem at Alcatraz was not the lack of support, it was the lack of Indian leadership. Drug and alcohol use among the occupiers became a major problem. Bernie and Joe knew that they could not allow this to happen in Seattle.

"Leadership has to be firm, Bernie," Joe had advised. "There can be little room for mistakes. Hundreds of people will come to support you.

Give them the leadership they deserve. If you are successful, you will change history. Indians have never gotten land back from whites once they took it. This will be a first."

Bernie remembered the many times they spoke of the problems that Indians were experiencing. Joe had a thorough understanding of tribes across the continent, and he spent a lot of time visiting other tribes. He rarely missed meetings or important conventions, regardless of the time or place. Joe was more than willing to share his knowledge with tribal leaders, hoping that it would help ease any conflict that existed between the tribe and state or federal agencies. Joe shared his important wisdom with Bernie.

"Bernie, it's important to maintain ties with the reservations," Joe counseled. "Indians are Indians no matter where they are forced to live. Many of them will still be a part of their tribe and their reservation no matter where they are living. Don't ever forget that."

Joe and Bernie had worked together for more than thirty years to fight for justice and fairness for Indians. Their paths had crossed many times in various parts of the country. There had never been two leaders who worked as closely and effectively as Joe DeLaCruz and Bernie Whitebear. They had traveled together to visit and to learn from other Indians who were having similar problems, on reservations and in urban Indian centers across the nation. When it came time to recreate, they spent hours in taverns toasting each other and enjoying each other's loyalty and company.

According to Joe, the Quinault Tribe's blueback salmon was the best-tasting salmon in the world. On Memorial Day each year, Joe and his family would travel up to the mountains in eastern Washington to Pia, where Bernie's ancestors were buried. There he would bake three dozen large bluebacks, Indian-style, for all to enjoy. I remember this show of consideration and generosity was always a highlight for the Lakes Indians on Memorial Day.

After Joe's passing, Bernie's condition deteriorated daily. Friends and supporters continued to visit. It was obvious that Bernie was suffering from the pain of his illness. He was also disturbed that he had to get around in a wheelchair. As the days went on, Bernie's mood changed and he would get angry if things did not go well or go his way. Everyone knew that Bernie was normally not this way. In the past he always made allowances for anyone's shortcomings. We all knew that time was short for him.

One day in June 2000 Bernie announced, quite unexpectedly, that he had decided to attend the board meeting for the National Museum of the American Indian in Washington, D.C. We were shocked and dead-set against Bernie making this trip. We felt he could not survive such an ordeal. Bernie's doctor was consulted in the hope he would rule against it. We were surprised when the doctor gave his consent. "It will be critical," the doctor said, "but I know how important this trip is to Bernie. It will be his last." Reluctantly, we consented. We were still deeply concerned he would not survive the journey.

Teresa, our younger sister, and a friend, Camille Mooney, were to travel with Bernie and watch over him. Flight arrangements were made and they departed on June 21. Bernie was able to attend two meetings at the Smithsonian but he was unable to attend the third and last meeting. He was too weak and frail. Before returning to Seattle, Bernie was able to visit the construction site of the future National Museum of the American Indian. He could envision the beautiful design of the structure in the Smithsonian complex. He was proud that he was one of many who had worked to see it become a reality. Bernie knew he would not live to see the completion of the museum, but he was pleased that he was a part of it.

Bernie smiled as he spoke of Douglas Cardinal, the Blackfoot architect who designed the building. He knew the Blackfoot Indians in Canada were directly related to the Blackfeet in the United States. They were once the most warlike warriors on the continent. Bernie was amused that one of the most beautiful structures in Washington, D.C., had been designed by a Blackfoot Indian, a direct descendant of those great warriors of the past.

When Bernie returned to Seattle, he was very weak. He could no longer walk without help. But he was content that he was able to make his last trip to Washington, D.C., to be with Rick West, Vine Deloria Jr., and the rest of the board members.

On July 9 family and friends planned another get-together and dinner. Everyone knew this would be Bernie's last. Several of Bernie's closest friends came. Bob and Sharon Tomeko Santos came to prepare chicken adobo, Bernie's favorite Filipino dish.

There were so many people that at least three dozen of Bernie's friends had to eat outside in Bernie's backyard. As they enjoyed their adobo they looked at six of Bernie's old cars that dominated the backyard. Repairing old cars had become a hobby for Bernie, a way of relieving stress. He came up with some of his best ideas while tinkering with engines and other parts of the cars. I was amused as his guests examined the cars in Bernie's backyard. They marveled at the numbers and vintage of the vehicles before them: a '71 Lincoln sedan, a '66 Mercury, a '64 Ford Mustang, a '75 Chevy van, a '66 Dodge pickup, and an ancient '48 MG Roadster.

As one of Bernie's friends studied the cars he remarked, "You can always tell if a person is an Indian by the number of old cars parked out in his yard. Go to any reservation and you'll see what I mean firsthand."

This seemed to be true of Bernie, in addition to the old cars in his yard, there were three others at the Daybreak Star Center and at least two in Pete Schnurman's backyard.

Suzie Chin, a close friend of Bernie's, brought a ukulele, hoping she could find someone to play it. I tuned it for her and strummed a few songs. I had not played a ukulele in over forty years, not since I was a young man. Throughout the afternoon people sang old familiar songs as I accompanied them on the ukulele.

Bernie sat majestically in the middle of his large leather sofa flanked by friends. I watched as he joined the singing, his eyes ever dark and flashing. It was obvious that he was enjoying this last time with his family and friends and he sang with gusto. From time to time Bernie requested that I give him a small tablet of morphine. He was in pain but he would not give in at this last important get-together. Everyone wanted to have a photograph taken with Bernie for the last time. Bernie smiled fondly as his great-nieces, Gaby and Recy, and his great-nephew, Duran, placed themselves close to him for one last photograph.

I walked over to Bernie and sat close by. He seemed to be preoccupied with the past. I listened as he quietly retraced the steps of his life. Bernie talked of the times with the Skins in Tacoma and how he learned of the difficulties urban Indians were having living in large cities away

Duran, Recy, and Gaby Reyes and Metis, El Sobrante, California, 2004.
Courtesy Darren and Helen Reyes

from their homelands. He reminded me of his experiences fishing for salmon with Bob Satiacum and his brothers, Buddy and Junior, on the Puyallup River and Commencement Bay in Tacoma. Bernie spoke of the harassment they faced from the state and white sportsmen. We laughed as we recalled Bob's arrogance and courage as he faced his enemy.

Bernie talked about the Nisqually Billy Frank Jr. and his involvement in the fish-ins on the Nisqually River. Bernie admired the courage that Billy Frank Jr. and his tribal members displayed as they resisted the invasions of their river by state authorities and white sportsmen who declared that all salmon were theirs. Bernie was proud that Billy became the chairman of the Northwest Indian Fisheries Commission after the Boldt Decision was passed in 1974 and that Billy was the recipient of the Albert Schweitzer Prize for Humanitarianism in 1991. Bernie took a slow deep breath. I could see that he was in pain, so I gave him a morphine tablet.

He continued reminiscing warmly about Janet McCloud, his close friend of the Tulalip Tribe. Her bravery on the Nisqually River as she and her family took part in the fish-ins was something to be proud of. Their determination was inspiring as they resisted attempts to be removed from the river. They would not be discouraged from taking their salmon. He spoke of his first meeting with her, when he wore the ragged loincloth he had fashioned for himself. We both laughed.

Bernie accepted a cup of green tea. He drank it slowly and started to talk about his friend, Vine Deloria Jr., the Standing Rock Sioux member. They first met in 1970, when Vine offered advice and support in getting land for the Indians in Seattle. Bernie knew that Vine had graduated in law and that Vine could write. Bernie talked of their good times as they sat on the board and exchanged ideas about the forthcoming National Museum of the American Indian in Washington, D.C. Bernie recalled Vine's book *Custer Died for Your Sins* and how it influenced his thinking and served as inspiration in fighting for Indian rights. Bernie spoke of the brilliance Vine exhibited when he chaired the National Congress of American Indians from 1964 to 1967.

Bernie's strength was beginning to fade, but his thoughts were still clear as he remembered his dear friend, Joe DeLaCruz. He told me of their many meetings in different parts of the country. He had always marveled at Joe's ability to define in-depth tribal issues that many of the leaders of those tribes failed to recognize. Bernie admired Joe's strong stance on tribal sovereignty for the Quinaults. He told me that he wished other tribes would follow Joe's thinking on the matter. Bernie felt that all tribes should take over the administration and planning of their business rather than depend on the U.S. government and the Bureau of Indian Affairs. Bernie had little patience with the history of the bureau. He felt that over the years the bureau had done little to improve their own image and involvement with the tribes they were supposed to help.

Bernie was weak and sleepy when he spoke of the struggles with the City of Seattle and the U.S. Army. I asked if he wanted to go to his bedroom, but he shook his head. Bernie studied me for a while and then with a grimace said, "Why the hell didn't you climb over the fence at Fort Lawton when you had the chance?" I smiled and shook my head. I told him someone had to remain outside to help bail out those who were thrown in the stockade. Bernie had never let me forget that I failed to go over the fence during the invasion. Over the years he let everyone who would listen know that I was there only to help push women like Ella Aquino, his old friend, and other elders over the fence.

He closed his eyes gently as he thought of the hundreds of Indians who came from many tribes to support him. He spoke of his beloved staff who worked with him over the years to make the UIATF a success. These good people, he told me, had become his best of friends.

Bernie talked of Vic Johns. He said that he appreciated his steadfastness and loyalty over the years. He considered himself lucky to have a friend such as Vic.

He spoke of Mom and Dad. He had loved and admired both of them all his life. He told me that all of us were fortunate to have such good parents. Bernie paused for a while and shared, "I will be seeing them soon, in another world."

Then he spoke of the issues at hand, the problems in Seattle. He told me that more had to be done to improve the conditions of our people. He whispered, "I wish there was more time for me to do this."

Bernie could sense the feeling of apprehension behind the smiling faces of his friends and family that night. Everyone was aware that a great era of purpose, effort, and accomplishment was ending. Everyone wanted to make this last day with Bernie memorable. They knew that they would never experience these good times again.

Bernie stayed up until the last of his friends left in the early evening. He was very tired and could barely keep his eyes open. He knew that he would never see them again. Family and friends remembered when the Associated Press interviewed Bernie a week earlier. The reporter asked him to sum up his lifetime. In a weak voice, he answered simply, "It was the best."

Luana and Kecia helped Bernie back to his bedroom for a well-needed rest.

"His influence and power will get stronger as
time goes by. He left us an extraordinary example."

—Roberto Maestas, director of El Centro de la Raza

Crossing Over

On July 14 Bernie could barely communicate. We sensed that time was short. We kept close watch over him. As he tried to raise his head at midday, Bernie murmured to Luana, "I think this is it." Those were the last words he spoke. Bernie closed his dark piercing eyes for the last time. He lingered for two more days, and his breathing was forced. It was obvious that he was fighting for his life. At one o'clock on July 16, 2000, Bernie crossed over. He simply stopped breathing. An important era for our family had ended. I stood at his bedside with Luana. We did not talk. Luana and I knew that the protective shield that had always covered the three of us was lifted.

That evening every television channel in Seattle covered Bernie's passing. The coverage was warm and sympathetic. There were photographs of Bernie that we had never seen. It was a heartfelt and wonderful tribute to a great leader. The next day there was front-page coverage of Bernie's death in the Seattle *Times* and the Seattle *Post-Intelligencer*. Reports of Bernie's passing were covered in newspapers throughout the nation and as far away as Hawaii, Japan, and Alaska. For the next two days Bernie received front-page coverage in the Seattle *Times*. It was as if the press could not let go of Bernie.

On July 20 a wake was held at the Daybreak Star Center. Hundreds of people attended. Many spoke and related stories about their times with Bernie. Many of the stories were humorous, some were heart wrenching. His simple wooden casket of ponderosa pine came from the Colville Indian Reservation. Bernie was laid to rest in his Green Beret

Recy Reyes, Teresa Wong, Darren Reyes, Luana Reyes, Laura Whitebear Wong, and Kecia Reyes stand behind Lawney Reyes as he speaks during the Bernie Whitebear memorial, 2000. *Courtesy John Loftus*

uniform. Many eagle feathers were placed in the coffin that night as the seven drums reverberated continuously, assisting Bernie in crossing over. People stepped up to the coffin and paid quiet tribute throughout the night. Star, Bernie's German Shepherd friend, appeared several times during the course of the night to check on Bernie. The sadness in his eyes was felt in the hearts of everyone.

The next day the memorial was held at the convention center in downtown Seattle. Sixteen Seattle police officers formed the motorcycle brigade followed by eight Harley Davidsons driven by Bernie's Muckleshoot friends. They led the hearse that carried Bernie's body. A caravan of cars carrying our family and friends followed. Two U.S. senators, Dan Inouye and Patty Murray, and two governors, Gary Locke and Mike Lowry, attended. King County Executive Ron Sims, Mayor Paul Schell, and Representative Jay Inslee were also present. State representatives, tribal leaders representing fifty-four tribes, and friends spoke to thousands of people in tribute to Bernie. John Daniels, the chairman of the Muckleshoot Tribe, was a pallbearer. Members of the tribe sat quietly as they paid silent tribute to an old friend.

At the end of the memorial our family was invited to the center stage. Some of us spoke about past times. Bernie's nephew, Darren, shared a favorite story about his uncle. Darren had made plans to attend his twenty-year reunion at the Lakeside School in Seattle. He told the large audience that Bernie asked if he could go in his place. Darren questioned Bernie, "Why would you want to do that?" Bernie, with wrinkles on his forehead and graying hair, answered, "I just wanted your classmates to know how hard it is to be an Indian." The large gathering laughed.

Laura, our youngest sister, was in tears. She ended the family's farewell address by saying: "Our family finds comfort in knowing that Bernie will be in the company of family and friends as he crosses over. We love you, Bernie. Have a good journey. Come visit us in our dreams."

The Mike Penney Drummers of the Nez Perce sang and drummed the beautiful "Old Warrior's Song" as Bernie's casket was taken from the large hall. What started as a heart-wrenching memorial ended as a heart-warming tribute to a respected leader. It was a good day to be Indian.

That night the annual pow wow was held at the Great Circle near the Daybreak Star Center. Thousands of people attended. Hundreds of singers, drummers, and dancers from many tribes performed. As the performances began, thunderclouds suddenly appeared in the sky above. At the first drumbeat from the lead drum, lightening flashed, followed by crashing thunder. Large raindrops fell as the audience and the performers tried to run for cover beneath vendor's tents. Within seconds the night sky cleared and the stars shone brightly above. Many regarded it as a signal from Bernie. It was a reminder that he was present for his last pow wow.

A month after Bernie's passing, Paul Schulz and I got together for coffee. We talked about the old days in Okanogan. Paul recalled the disturbing morning when his mother called Bernie a "Siwash." A hint of tears appeared briefly in his eyes as he related the story once again. He was amazed by Bernie's many accomplishments in life. Finally, he said softly, "That little SOB went a long way. I'll miss him."

A few weeks afterward Dennis and Pat Key, Bernie's close friends now living in East Wenatchee, wrote me a letter and shared other experiences they had with Bernie when they went to school together in Okanogan. When they were invited to attend Bernie's tribute at Union Station in 1997, they came expecting to see a small gathering of Bernie's family and close friends. They stood in awe at the size of the Union Station and the hundreds of people already seated in the large banquet hall. They could not believe that so many officials representing the city, state, and federal governments would be there, seated next to so many leaders of Indian tribes from across the nation. The numbers of ethnic groups present surprised Dennis and Pat. After listening to the many tributes to Bernie, Pat shared, "I felt so proud of Bernie that night and of having the chance to know him when we were young."

After the tribute, Dennis found the nearest telephone and called his mother long distance. He wanted to tell her that, contrary to her predictions of so long ago, Bernard had finally amounted to something. Dennis mused as his mother listened. He sensed her difficulty in believing what he was saying about that little Indian, the one who used to drive that old '34 Ford Coupe. With some effort she remembered the car. She remembered the damaged muffler. Mrs. Key remembered that it made a lot of noise, late in the night, around the little town of Malott.

Bernie Whitebear, Luana Reyes, Lawney Reyes, and Kecia Reyes, Walnut Creek, California, 1991. *Courtesy Darren Reyes and Rebecca Pabrua Reyes*

Bernie Whitebear and Washington Governor Gary Locke, Olympia, ca. 1996. *Courtesy Gary Locke*

Bernie Whitebear at the Great Circle, Daybreak Star Center, 1985.
Courtesy Randy J. McDougall

Jamie Garner,
Seattle, 2002.
*Courtesy Jamie
Garner*

Mike Lowry,
former governor
of Washington.
Courtesy Mike Lowry

Stephanie Meachem (front), Harry Wong, Teresa Wong, Lara Lin Reyes, and Kecia Reyes (back), Seattle, 1978. *Courtesy Joyce Meachem Reyes*

Bernie (right) at Ft. Campbell, Kentucky in 1959 with Bob Perry (left) and two other members of his army unit, Company D, 501st Battle Group, 101st Airborne Division. *Courtesy Robert B. Perry, Ozark, Missouri*

Epilogue

Bernie Whitebear had many setbacks in life. He was sometimes discouraged by his opposition, but he never voiced negative comments about them. He would simply pick himself up, regain his stance, and continue to work and fight for what he thought was right for his people. He did this continuously for nearly forty years. Because of this, his opponents might disagree with him on certain issues but they never regarded or thought of Bernie Whitebear in a negative light. There was always a sense of respect.

Everyone had a favorite story about Bernie. He had a spontaneous wit and he could make anyone laugh. Judy Leask Guthrie, who worked for the UIATF, told me that once her brother came to visit her at the Daybreak Star Center. He was six foot two and good looking, and many agreed he resembled the actor Tom Selleck. Judy brought her brother over to Bernie and introduced him. Bernie shook his hand as he looked up at him and said, "There was a time, not too long ago, when I looked just like you." After a brief silence everyone broke out into uncontrollable laughter. Judy told friends that when her family had a reunion, five years later, Bernie's words still brought down the house.

A large get-together to honor Bernie was held at the Daybreak Star Center in 1998. Bernie got up to speak and thank the three hundred people who had attended. He was completely bald because of the effects of chemotherapy. Bernie announced, "Joe DeLaCruz called me the other day and asked if I would go in halves with him on a bottle of Viagra. I paused for a minute, then told him that I would have to take a rain-check because I had heard that it affects your memory negatively. I told Joe that I was afraid that I might have a good time and not be able to remember it."

Over the years other humorous stories were told of Bernie's life and adventures. Claudia Kauffman, the deputy manager of the Daybreak Star Center, shared the following story, perhaps one of the best.

One morning as Bernie drove to work at the Daybreak Star Center he heard a newsflash on his car radio. He heard the announcer say that a thousand Cherokees were surrounding the nation's Capitol in Washington, D.C. The radio was not working well and there was a lot of static. Bernie was excited that Indians were on the warpath. He would purchase airline tickets immediately and fly back to support the Cherokees. He wanted to be a part of what he envisioned the last great Indian War in the nation. Excitedly, he called his staff on his cell phone and asked them to turn on the television to a news channel. He was on his way and would be there in minutes.

Bernie arrived at the Daybreak Star Center, jumped out of his car, and ran to the entrance. One of his staff advised, "Relax, Bear, the newsman was not talking about Cherokees, he was talking about cherry trees. A thousand cherry trees surrounding the nation's Capitol." Bernie shook his head and walked to his office somewhat confused and disappointed. He murmured, "Cherry trees? I could have sworn they were talking about Cherokees."

After his passing Bernie received other awards, which were presented to the family. In 2000 the City of Seattle awarded Bernie the Distinguished Citizen Medal, and the University of Washington presented Bernie an Outstanding Alumnus Award. At a special tribute in San Francisco, Bernie received the American Indian Film Festival Award. In 2001 the Seattle *Times* designated Bernie as one of one hundred fifty people who made the greatest impact on Seattle during the last one hundred fifty years. This was followed by proclamations awarded to Bernie by the Seattle City Council, the King County Council, and the House of Representatives in Olympia. As a special tribute from old friends, Peter and Hinda Schnurman had seven trees planted in Israel in 2000, as a living memorial to Bernie Whitebear.

Luana Reyes, director of Headquarters Operations, Indian Health Service, Rockville, Maryland, 1990. *Courtesy Indian Health Services*

The board of directors of the UIATF have agreed to dedicate themselves to getting the proposal of the People's Lodge accepted by the city. They are aware that this was important to Bernie as his final gift to the Indian people. They want their efforts, in turn, to be a gift from the people to Bernie. The board plans to name the building The Bernie Whitebear People's Lodge.

Fifteen months after Bernie died, Luana, after returning from a visit to Italy, became ill with sudden-onset aplastic anemia. She went into the Georgetown University Hospital in Washington, D.C., for treatment. I flew to be with her. After struggling with the illness for less than a month, she passed away. Our family was stunned. It was unimaginable that this could happen so soon after the loss of our brother.

Bob Morrisson, Doyne Alward, and Therese Kennedy Johns with
"Dreamcatcher," Yesler Way and 32nd Street, Seattle, 2003.
Courtesy Therese Kennedy Johns

While Luana was in the hospital fighting for her life, President George W. Bush awarded her the Presidential Rank Meritorious Award, accompanied by a check for twenty-five thousand dollars.

During her years as the director of headquarters operations for Indian Health Service, Luana made major improvements to the quality of healthcare for Indians throughout the nation. Everyone Luana met loved and respected her. The name of the new Indian Health Service headquarters building in Rockville, Maryland, was named The Reyes Building in her honor.

Months later Jill Marsden and Ros Bond, close friends of Bernie and Luana, thought that a memorial would be fitting for the two in Seattle. They asked me if I would do this for my brother and sister. Everyone who knew them agreed they were both dreamers who made their dreams come true for the benefit of Indian people. I consented and came up with the design of "Dreamcatcher," a stainless steel memorial that stands twenty feet high.

A year later funds were raised through the efforts of Therese Kennedy Johns, Joan Singler, and Laura Wong Whitebear. More than one hundred fifty donors contributed to the costs of the fabrication and installation of "Dreamcatcher." It was completed and installed at Yesler Way and 32nd Street in Seattle on July 19, 2003. The Seattle *Times* and the television stations in Seattle covered the dedication as hundreds came to pay tribute. It was a special honor for me to have the privilege of designing "Dreamcatcher" for my sister and brother.

On October 7, 2003, people gathered in the Okanogan High School auditorium for a special assembly to honor three extraordinary graduates: Bernie, Luana, and me. More than three hundred and fifty students, friends, and classmates were there. Principal Tom Monroe read a proclamation from Governor Gary Locke honoring the event. Ella Wylet Schreckengost, Luana's best friend, served as the mistress of ceremonies. She and Janice Burnett Mitzner, another friend of Luana's, organized the event. Ella shared high school memories with the student body. JoAnne Kauffman, a Nez Perce who succeeded Luana as the executive director of the Seattle Indian Health Board, was the main speaker. She was a longtime friend of our family. She covered the struggles and accomplishments of Bernie and Luana during their days in

Seattle. At the end of the assembly, I retraced our family's times on the Colville Reservation, when we were youngsters. I told of the everyday life and struggles our family endured before coming to Okanogan. At the end of my talk, the student body rose and gave a standing ovation.

Several of the programs Bernie originated still exist today, providing ongoing services to those who need them. Fundraising is still a difficult challenge. Time has proven that it is difficult to find individuals who are gifted at this. Since Bernie's passing the UIATF has suffered. Funding grants have been reduced, making it impossible to retain staff and maintain important programs. There does not seem to be the magnet that attracts Indians and non-Indians to the Daybreak Star Center. The spirit of the building and grounds is quiet, and there is little activity or community action or involvement with others. The unfortunate departure of the talented grant writers and staff has made it nearly impossible to continue in the tradition that once was. It seemed that UIATF was in its twilight, signaling the end of those great days. Recognizing this, certain members of the Board of Directors enlisted an old friend of Bernie's, Phil Lane Jr., a Yankton Dakota-Chickasaw, to correct this problem. As the interim director Phil displayed some of the same intelligence and energy that Bernie once had.

After Bernie's passing W. Richard West, director of the National Museum of the American Indian in Washington, D.C., stated in an interview with Debra Crain, "There is just a wonderful consistency through time. Bernie never really changed. He just got bigger and bigger in life as he went along. He was such a good individual with great character and warmth. He was out at the very edge, lots of times, of what was going on in the Indian world and yet was always so constructive and positive about it . . . and that is a rare gift."

Accolades

Someone once asked, "How do you judge greatness?" Another replied, "By a wide cross section of appraisal by others." If that is true, one might consider the following.

"Bernie was soft spoken but outspoken." — Bob Santos, director of Inter*Im, Seattle

"A little bear with a big bite." — Melissa Lin, *Asian American Journal*, Seattle

"He persuaded others to do what they ought to do." — Mike Layton, Seattle *Post-Intelligencer*

"My ultimate memory of him is as one of the kindest and gentlest. He was the most humorous person I had dealt with. He never lost his sense of humor. I visited him on St. Patrick's Day. He was planning his own funeral." — Tom Keefe, attorney and friend, Spokane

"You could always depend on him to be there to help you."
— Larry Gossett, executive director of Central Area Motivation Program, Seattle

"The Bear's legacy is that his Indian People could dance, gather, laugh, and share."—Mike Smith, director of the American Indian Film Festival, San Francisco

"Bernie fought to improve the quality of life of Indian People during a time when it was contrary to the status quo. I regard him as my own personal hero."—Dan Evans, former governor and U.S. Senator, Washington

"I met Bernie at a pow wow at the University of Washington. I told him I could stay for only a few minutes because of an important meeting. He had me dance with hundreds of Indians. Two hours later I left."—Patty Murray, U.S. Senator, Washington

"Bernie has achieved three times more in life than anyone I know." —Erland Lau, friend, Seattle

"Wherever you go in Indian Country, there is always one name that is remembered, Bernie Whitebear."—Ralph Forquera, executive director of the Seattle Indian Health Board

"He would give you confidence to stand up, speak out, and persevere."—Mike Quill, teenager, I' Wa' Sil, United Indians of All Tribes Foundation

"I want you to know I regard you equal to any of the great Chiefs." —Wendy Tokuda, Channel 5 TV, San Francisco

"He was a dreamer. He was a great leader. Bernie was known from the State of Washington to the City of Washington." —Daniel Inouye, U.S. Senator, Hawaii

"He had a Gandhi-like quality. He was truly the Citizen of the Century in the State of Washington."—Gary Locke, former governor of the State of Washington

"Bernie once said, 'It was wrong of the United States to not uphold Indian Fishing Rights in Washington State. Great nations, like great men, must keep their word.'"—Mike Lowry, former governor of the State of Washington

"Bernie regarded life and work as the same thing."
—Alex Tizon, Seattle *Times*

"Bernie was not only the Executive Director of the United Indians of All Tribes Foundation, he *was* the United Indians of All Tribes Foundation."—Joe DeLaCruz, director of the Quinault Tribe

"To me Bernie Whitebear was the type of leader that I respected the most."—Janet McCloud, Tulalip Indian activist

"Bernie was a real leader. He was my mentor."
—Phil Lane Jr., Yankton Dakota-Chickasaw activist

"All the way up to Thursday he was meeting with people. His body was getting weaker and weaker but his mind was still going a hundred miles an hour."—Claudia Kauffman, deputy manager of Daybreak Star Center

"The Daybreak Star Center is known among Indians as 'the house that Bernie built.' He traveled a long way from his family's canvas tent to that house, and Native Americans all over the region say they are better for it."—Joshua Robin and Warren King, Seattle *Times*

"Whitebear never lost his sense of life as play, no matter how serious. Yet he stood by his convictions. He was driven to help his people, and the world finally came around to his doorstep."—Mike Dillon, *Queen Anne News*, Seattle

"Bernie was as passionate about justice and dignity for all people as he was for sovereignty and self-determination for Native Americans.

He was a tireless, charismatic fighter, known and loved by all who knew him. While his physical presence may be gone, his spirit continues to live within each and every one of us."—Jamie Garner, attorney for the UIATF

"No one helped more Indians in need in the last century than Bernie Whitebear."—Vine Deloria Jr., respected Lakota attorney, writer, and educator, Boulder, Colorado

"The world lost a great man on July 16, 2000, Bernard Julian Whitebear."—Debra A. Crain, Smithsonian Institution, Washington, D.C.

"The Indian People in Seattle are blessed to have a leader such as Bernie Whitebear. He has always been here for them."
—Vi Hilbert, respected elder of the Upper Skagit Tribe

"The way Bernie was, you'd come around to Daybreak Star, you'd see all these people here, dressed up and you'd go, 'Hey, where's Bernie?' And he'd be right there, doing the salmon."
—Richard Restoule, longtime friend

"He could go anywhere, with the politicians, tribal leaders, and with everyday people."—Victor Johns, friend

"Bernie was a little man but he had a big heart."—George Meachem, Yakama and Swinomish Tribe member and friend

"Bernie once said all that really counts on this earth is that we all do the best we can . . . and, *my*, how he did that."—Mike Lowry, former governor of the State of Washington

"He was my little brother. He did a lot for American Indians. I'm proud of him."—Lawney Reyes, older brother in Channel 9 TV interview

"Bernie Whitebear was more than just an Indian leader who happened to inhabit the Seattle civic scene. His recent passing leaves a void in the community at large. He was a man who got things done. Unlike many who rise to the top of the civic affairs heap, he accomplished his goals through good humor and a respect for the feelings, ideas, and beliefs of others.

I am one of hundreds, maybe thousands, who liked to think of Bernie as a close personal friend. We knew each other first as soldiers. Later, as a political reporter for the *Post-Intelligencer* in Olympia, I watched Bernie as he developed a persona as a public figure, perfecting his innate skill in persuading others to do what they ought to do.

Bernie and I met when he was released from active duty by the Army with a reserve obligation. He had been a paratrooper in the 101st Airborne Division. I was commanding an Army Special Forces team (nicknamed Green Beret) based in South Tacoma, and I welcomed this soft-spoken, smiling man. He became the weapons specialist in my team. I had known many good soldiers as a paratrooper in two wars, and Bernie was equal to any of them.

He was a morale booster, always ready with a quip or a song. Once a month, the team gathered for a weekend of instruction and we'd run five miles. Bernie led in singing the Army's Jody cadence song, very popular with other team members.

Shortly after Bernie's arrival, we went to the Wasatch Mountains in Utah for our annual two-week summer training. Bernie celebrated rather heavily the night before we were to leave, and two friends brought him to the Tacoma armory in pretty sad condition. But he brought his rucksack, presumably with his sleeping bag, extra boots, and gear and a duffle bag with extra clothing for the cool mountains.

We flew to Salt Lake City and were trucked high up into the Wasatch range and then marched five miles beyond the trailhead where we made camp. Bernie opened his rucksack and, to our surprise—and his—it contained only a basketball, inflated, an 8-mm camera, and a bugle. His duffle bag was stuffed with dirty laundry.

Bernie, wearing thin civilian summer clothing, volunteered to do most of the night guard duty, wearing three T-shirts, because it was too cold to sleep. He snatched naps now and then between patrols during the days.

We were practicing guerrilla warfare against another Special Forces reserve outfit from Southern California, which was chiefly made up of L.A. cops and deputy sheriffs, tough guys but uniformly 20 pounds overweight. Bernie was a superb scout and he could run up and down mountains all day. The L.A. cops could never catch us with Bernie.

At the end of the first week, we set up an ambush with blank ammunition and M-80 firecrackers on a trail the L.A. cops would have to take up the side of a broad valley. I asked Bernie if he could play a tune on his bugle.

Well, maybe 'Taps' he said. How about 'Charge'? He would try . . . but no rehearsal. So we took cover upslope from the trail and watched as the plump cops toiled upward, squirting sweat from every pore. We let their scouts clump on up the trail and when their main body was just below us, I nodded to Bernie.

His version of 'Charge' echoed back and forth across the valley, the notes punctuated by blank rifle fire. The boys from L.A. did standing broad jumps down the side of the mountain, losing packs and rifles on the way.

We retired over on our side of the mountain, only stopping to catch a breath for laughing, and went down the mountain to chute up for a parachute jump, which Bernie captured by tying his camera to his foot and recording the swirling world around him.

When Bernie's reserve time was up, he let his hair grow and swore off the sauce. He became a lobbyist in Olympia. I introduced Bernie to key legislators, sometimes giving him my assessment of their character and ability. One of these was Sen. Hubert Donohue, a Franklin County wheat farmer and Chairman of the Ways and Means Committee who most people believed had a heart the size of a grain of wheat and just as hard.

But Bernie had a dream of what was to become the Daybreak Star Center in Fort Lawton. He needed matching money to make it a reality and he went to work, with his soft Indian voice and little boy's smile, on hard-hearted Hubert Donohue.

He got his money.

Olympia old-timers were astounded. Over the years Bernie melted other hearts, becoming one of the smoothest schmoozers in the state. He didn't need my help any more. Bernie wore his fame lightly, modestly, and while he collected chits everywhere, he never seemed to be using anyone.

We need more Bernie Whitebears in this nearly leaderless community."—Mike Layton, Commanding Officer of Special Forces Team (Green Beret) and guest columnist, Seattle *Post-Intelligencer*

Acknowledgments

Over the years my dad, Julian, shared many stories about our family that enabled me to write about our early years together. When I discovered my mother Mary's diary after her passing, it brought back other memories I had forgotten. Without this important information from my dad and mother, the story of my brother's early childhood would have been incomplete.

I want to thank Dennis and Pat Barnes Key for their input about Bernie's junior high and high school years in Okanogan. Their help enabled me to place key information in the manuscript to complete the circle of Bernie's life. Marilyn Hodgson, Paul Schulz, Doris Myers Reynolds, and Delores Myers Patterson—"the magpies"—Bernie's close friends, also contributed important information about Bernie's teenage years. All were his classmates and an important part of his life.

Peter Schnurman provided insight regarding the politics and fundraising that paid for the programs and the salaries of staff of the United Indians of All Tribes Foundation (UIATF). Jamie Garner, the attorney who worked with Bernie for fourteen years, shared important information regarding the agencies that provided funding for the acquisition of properties for the UIATF. He also enlightened me on some of Bernie Whitebear's long-term goals that were not realized before his death. I wish to give thanks to Jill Marsden who offered information about the work of the volunteers who were instrumental in forming the Seattle Indian Health Board. Over the years Peter, Jamie, and Jill helped Bernie immensely in formulating and administering to the needs of the Indian people in Seattle.

It was also my good fortune to have the help of Bob Morrisson. With his expertise and computer skills, photographs that were old and not in the best of condition were brought to new life.

When I encountered difficulty in writing the manuscript Therese Kennedy Johns, my friend, was always there to help. She deserves all the credit for researching, arranging, and editing the manuscript. Weeks, months, and finally years of dedicated effort were devoted by Therese to bring it to completion.

Finally, I want to thank my copyeditor, Lisa DiDonato, for adding fine and important passages to the overall manuscript.

Bibliography

American Friends Service Committee. 1970. *Uncommon Controversy*: *Fishing Rights of the Muckleshoot, Puyallup, and Nisqually Indians*. Seattle: University of Washington Press.

Bicentennial Association. 1976. *From Pioneers to Power*: *Historical Sketches of the Grand Coulee Dam Area*. Colville, Wash.: The Statesman-Examiner, Inc.

Chance, David H. 1986. *People of the Falls*. Colville: Kettle Falls Historical Center.

Cody, Robin. 1995. *Voyage of a Summer Sun*: *Canoeing the Columbia River*. New York: Alfred A. Knopf.

DeLaCruz, Joe. 1998. *Testimony on Behalf of the Quinault Indian Nation, U.S. Senate Committee on Indian Affairs Field Hearings, Senate Bill 1691*. Seattle: Tribal Sovereignty Immunity.

Deloria, Vine, Jr. 1969. *Custer Died for Your Sins*: *An Indian Manifesto*. New York: Macmillan.

Hardin, Blaine. 1996. *A River Lost*: *The Life and Death of the Columbia*. New York: W. W. Norton & Company.

Lakin, Ruth. 1976. *Kettle River Country*: *Early Days along the Kettle River*. Colville, Wash.: The Statesman-Examiner, Inc.

Miller, Jay, ed. 1990. *Mourning Dove*: *A Salishan Autobiography*. Lincoln: University of Nebraska Press.

Reyes, Lawney L. 2002. *White Grizzly Bear's Legacy*: *Learning to Be Indian*. Seattle: University of Washington Press.

Index

ABOUT THE AUTHOR

After his birth in Bend, Oregon, in 1931 Lawney Reyes's family moved to the Colville Indian Reservation, where their people lived. There he spent his young years growing and learning about the land, the wildlife, and the people that were a part of it. In the summer of 1944 his family moved to Okanogan, Washington, where he worked in the apple orchards and went to high school.

Reyes moved to Seattle and attended the University of Washington, where he received a bachelor's degree in interior design in 1959. He spent two years in the U.S. Army stationed in Germany. He then worked as the interior designer for the Seafirst Corporation for fourteen years and was appointed the corporate art director. Over the next seven years he created a corporate art collection for Seafirst.

In his free time, he created many sculptures commissioned by corporations throughout the United States, Europe, and Asia. He has won numerous awards for his sculpture in Washington, D.C., and in the Southwest. In Washington, he was honored with the Governor's Art Award in 1972 and the Peace and Friendship Award in 1982. In 2002 Reyes's first book, *White Grizzly Bear's Legacy*, was published by the University of Washington Press.

He currently lives in Seattle, where he writes, sculpts, and spends time with his three grandchildren, Gaby, Recy, and Duran. He is also writing a book about B Street, the building of the Grand Coulee Dam, and its effect on the Columbia River and the lives that bordered it.

Lawney Reyes working on a model of "Dreamcatcher," Seattle, 2002. *Courtesy Seattle Times*